Praise f
Your Best Happi

"Ginger Kolbaba, in her uniq
style, opens her arms to tho.
and offers them a new look at fairy tales and
renewed hope. With refreshing vulnerability,
Ginger encourages women to set their eyes on
the eternal Bridegroom so they can experience
His joy in a new way."
>—SHEILA SEIFERT, Editorial Director of Parenting,
>*Thriving Family*, Focus on the Family

"Reading *Your Best Happily Ever After* was like
spending time with an encouraging girlfriend
over coffee! Speaking straight to our princess
hearts, Ginger Kolbaba uses humor and great
insights to help us discover God's incredible love
for each of us. Curl up with a warm mug and get
ready to enjoy!"
>—SHERRY SURRATT, CEO and President,
>MOPS International

"Ginger Kolbaba spins happily-ever-after tales into
both practical and spiritual examinations of how
our hearts can find happiness. . . . This book digs
deeper than ball gowns and fairy godmothers.
It's rich with scripture and stories from the Bible
and her own personal experience, helping us
understand God's true desire for our own happy
ending, not to mention the day-to-day joy we
desperately desire. . . .Highly recommended!"
>—RENE GUTTERIDGE, author of *Old Fashioned*

"*Your Best Happily Ever After* is a whimsical balance of wisdom and entertainment. . . . It will encourage you, strengthen your resolve, and make you feel as though you can ride your own white horse into a happily-ever-after designed just for you."

—DEBBIE JANSEN, family specialist and author of *Scriptures against Abuse*

"If you've ever been disappointed, disillusioned, or discouraged, then Ginger Kolbaba's words are for you. Life may not be a fairy tale, but it can still be full of hope, redemption, and adventure with the God who is our ultimate true love. We're part of a deeper, wilder story than we can even imagine, and the best is yet to come."

—HOLLEY GERTH, bestselling author of *You're Already Amazing*

"With wonderful wit and wisdom, Ginger Kolbaba weaves fairy-tale wonder, real-life struggles, and timeless biblical nuggets of hope that move a reader toward her own "happily ever after." *Your Best Happily Ever After* is a delight to read. . .but even better, a delight to apply to our own love stories!"

—PAM FARREL, author of 40 books including bestselling *Men Are Like Waffles, Women Are Like Spaghetti* and *Red Hot Monogamy*

"Embracing a happy life includes dealing with the poisoned apples, toxic people, and our own disappointing fairy tales. Ginger shows us how to rewrite our stories by developing resilience, taking more risks, and accepting our uniqueness. I'm so grateful for her support to fully live the best years of our lives!"

—MELINDA SCHMIDT, Midday Connection talk show, *Bring To Mind* podcast, Moody Radio, Chicago

"We all long for happiness, but we all deal with the hard stuff of life at one time or another. How do we balance the "happily ever after" dream with the reality of life? Ginger lovingly shows us how on the pages of this book. I loved it, and I know you will too!"

—JILL SAVAGE, CEO of Hearts at Home and author *No More Perfect Moms*

"Don't believe the lie that misery is next to godliness! Ginger shows us that God loves laughing over us and wants us to giggle, too! Here's her happiness roadmap—using fairy tales as her guide—to show us that we can catch hold of that abundant life. But we won't find happiness by pasting a plastic smile to our faces. We'll find it by growing up and being honest before God—and ourselves. So don't make stupid decisions. Be God's princess and live happily-ever-after instead!"

—SHEILA WRAY GREGOIRE, author of *9 Thoughts That Can Change Your Marriage*

YOUR BEST

Happily Ever After

Loving God's
Beautiful Story
for Your Life

GINGER KOLBABA

SHILOH RUN PRESS
An Imprint of Barbour Publishing, Inc.

Contents

Chapter 1

ONCE UPON A TIME

*So let us come boldly to the throne
of our gracious God. There we will
receive his mercy, and we will find grace
to help us when we need it most.*

HEBREWS 4:16 NLT

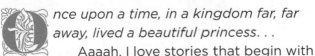

nce upon a time, in a kingdom far, far away, lived a beautiful princess. . .

Aaaah. I love stories that begin with "Once upon a time." As soon as I hear or read those magical, mystical words, I instinctively draw in a sharp breath of anticipation. For I know, indeed I'm certain, that an adventure is going to take place. Throughout the story, the heroine will encounter dragons and poisoned apples, dwarfs and talking donkeys, singing bluebirds and lost stilettos. Yet I can be assured throughout her journey that no matter what happens—whatever an evil stepmother, flying monkey, or overweight, horned-back sea monster does to spoil the protagonist's dreams—ultimately I know the ending. Because the beginning gives it away.

The heroine wins the day. She gets her prince charming. The bad guys get their dues. And everyone lives. . .(spoiler alert) happily ever after. That's the thing we've come to expect from "Once upon a time" stories: *Cinderella. Snow White. Sleeping Beauty. Shrek.* They always end with: "And they lived happily ever after."

We sigh and smile and know that's what we want for our lives—that chance for a happily ever after. For all our dreams to come true. For us to be happy and healthy and witty and loved. And having a fairy godmother with a magic wand certainly wouldn't hurt.

Too often, unfortunately, our existence feels more like a season of *Downton Abbey*—which is anything *but* living happily ever after. We're just on the verge of bliss and life shatters down around us once again.

Happily ever after is reserved for fairy tales, yes? They are escapist legends meant to add a little pleasure, excitement, and dare I say, repetitive, hummable songs to our mundane lives. If *only* we could break out into song backed by a chorus of cute, harmless forest creatures singing in perfect harmony. If only we had a magic wand to help us clean our houses and domesticated mice to sew Oscar-worthy gowns to fit our perfect size 2 bodies. If only the prince were always charming and handsome and witty and loyal. If only. . .

As Christians, of course, we know of a *true* story that begins with "Once upon a time." It states, "In the beginning. . ."

Genesis chapter 1, verse 1 starts out right away with that air of anticipation. As I read those words, I feel myself instinctively draw in a sharp breath. For I know, indeed I'm certain, that an adventure is going to take place.

In the beginning. . .

Throughout the story, the heroes and heroines will encounter swarms of locusts and cursed fruit, giants and talking donkeys, parted seas and stairways to heaven. Yet I can be assured throughout their journey that no matter what happens—whatever an evil relation, Passover angel of death, or hair-cutting wench does to spoil the protagonist's dreams—ultimately I know the ending. Because the beginning gives it away.

Prince Charming shows up and rescues the heroine. The bad guys get their dues. And everyone lives. . .(Bible spoiler alert) happily ever after. That's the thing we've come to expect from "In the beginning." It always ends with: "And they lived happily ever after."

This is no new revelation for you, I'm sure. If you're like me, you've heard that analogy a thousand and one times.

We know it in our heads. We hear it at church or among our Christian friends. Jesus wins the battle. He makes everything work for good, and someday when we die, we get to go to heaven and live forever, where there will be no more tears or sadness or death or school loan payments or annoying neighbors or size 14 dresses *or* calories. Hallelujah and thank you, God.

But heaven seems a long way away. Years, *decades*, hopefully. And while heaven is wonderful, earth has more than its share of trouble and heartache. So what do we do in the meantime? What do we do while we're waiting out the happily-ever-after part? While we're living in an adventure that often may feel as though we're stuck in the middle of a Disney ride, listening to small globally minded children wail, "It's a small world after all," over and over and. . . ?

Do we suffer in silence while we wait to be rescued? Wear the mantle of martyr and give in to depression, sadness, and filthy dwarfs messing up our living rooms? Do we pretend that everything is great when really our magic mirror is cracked and looks more like it belongs in a carnival fun house?

We could. But then we might end up being more closely aligned with the silly stepsisters instead of Cinderella.

The good news is that we don't have to give in. We can actually experience happily ever after right now. With a little encouragement from some fairy-tale writers, along with some wise biblical authors, we can pursue a joy-filled life today. And wonderfully enough, it's with the kind of spiritual "magic" we don't need a wand to receive. Too good to be true?

Here's the secret: we have within us all the "magic" we need to make our lives matter, to find lasting contentment, and to experience God in ways we've never imagined.

So why don't we clue in to it? In my work and travels I've met hundreds of women who want to grab hold of all the fairy-tale dreams, but they don't. They remain befuddled, continuing to be the cinder girl instead of going to the ball and trying on the Manolos made specifically for them. Why?

How We Get It Wrong

I was fortunate to work on three national magazines that I loved: *Today's Christian Woman, Marriage Partnership*, and *Kyria*.[1] I got to read the best of the best writing and work with the best of the best authors. Most days it was a blast.

But part of my job included reading e-mails, letters, and blog comments from readers and articles from potential authors who struggled with overwhelming pain. Their worlds were consumed with drudgery and, sadly, hopelessness. There was no happy life today and no happily ever after on the horizon for them. They couldn't see past the point of current circumstances and slowly, eventually, they gave up. They stopped truly believing that God was on their side, working behind the scenes on their behalf. They forgot that the Holy Spirit dwelling within them was actually there for a purpose and not simply hanging out waiting for eternity to begin. I would read their words and deeply feel their ache.

One letter in particular grabbed my attention. The reader wrote that she and her husband lived like roommates, that she used to try to spice up the romance, but her marriage was lifeless. Though I'd read similar stories from dozens of other women, this woman's writing was straightforward and dead. It was as though I could hear the flat-lined heart in her words.

I placed the letter on my desk (in those days we still wrote with the archaic paper and pen), walked to my office door, shut it, returned to my chair, and sobbed. I cried for this woman—and for all the women who had done everything "right" in their relationships, their jobs, their finances—and who still suffered. I sobbed because I had also suffered pain in my past, and while the circumstances were different, I could sympathize with the feelings. But I also sobbed because these wonderful, beautiful, priceless women hadn't moved beyond the pain yet. In a sense, they were held captive in the tower, waiting for a prince to come—who seemed to have gotten detoured somewhere around Albuquerque and might not show up at all.

I'll be the first to admit that keeping our

eyes focused on the happily-ever-after ending of heaven can be difficult when we're facing a menopausal dragon who is a dead ringer for our boss, a health crisis that nobody seems to want to get to the root of, or a relationship that offers romance in the form of betrayal. It's tough to consider pursuing happiness—or even having it pursue us!—when we're in the middle of a string of no-good, really terrible weeks. We just want to be left alone, have a moment of peace, and enjoy a genuine laugh like we haven't for a long time. Is that too much to ask?

The Two Extremes to Happily Ever After

Too often we listen too closely to one of two camps bellowing their opinions on the idea of living happily ever after every day. The first camp argues that, above all, God wants us to be happy. He's a good God and he wants good things for us. So we must pursue with abandon those things that bring us happiness (and success, wealth, fame, perfect children, perfect casseroles). Since God is love and a big part of love means feeling happy, it stands to reason that happiness is the endgame.

The other camp argues that we mustn't focus on happiness, for this life is filled with hardship and sacrifice. God isn't interested in our happiness; he's interested in our holiness. If you catch a glimpse of happiness, great, but don't pursue it.

Both camps are wrong.

Does God want us to be happy? Emphatically, I say yes.

Does God want us to be holy? Emphatically, I say yes.

Is it possible to be both? Again . . . yes, oh yes, and I'm not just wishing on a star.

Here's the problem when we go extreme in our pursuit of the happily ever after: we go extreme in our pursuit. In other words, we narrowly define what God wants for us and how we should respond, when there's room for complexity and a wide array of colors of emotions and thoughts. God isn't so black-and-white with his gifts and adventures for us. He desires for us to experience happiness *and* holiness. And I can tell you personally, it is possible to experience them at the same time. But we're getting ahead of ourselves. First let's break down what's wrong with each of these camps.

CAMP 1: GOD WANTS ME TO BE HAPPY ABOVE ALL.

God is a God of joy. He anointed Jesus with

the oil of joy (Hebrews 1:9). And since we are called to be Christlike, it's okay for us to pursue joy and happiness. Jesus loved to laugh—after all, children flocked around him, and kids don't tend to enjoy being around grumpies. So it makes sense that God wants our happiness. He designed us with the emotion of "happy," so of course he delights in us using it.

Think about that for a minute. When we're happy, we live in the present, taking in and experiencing the excitement of that moment. How can we not be happy when we watch a puppy trip over his too-big paws or when we see a duck in a pond with his little bottom and tail feathers sticking straight up in the air? Those things make me happy—and I believe they make God happy, too.

How do I know they make God happy? Because in Psalm 104:26 I read, "See the ships sailing along, and Leviathan, which you made to play in the sea" (NLT). Another translation says "formed to frolic there" (NIV). I love the word *frolic*.

Several years ago, I visited Chicago's Shedd Aquarium and watched the beluga whales. A baby was swimming around with its mama and another adult whale. As I stood at the glass, Baby Beluga blew out a series of bubbles from its blow hole and then swam quickly around to grab as many as it could in its mouth. Even the adults got in on the fun. I could sense that they were all playing and enjoying themselves. They were happy!

God created them to do that. He is a happy God, so of course it stands to reason that he delights when his creation rejoices in life.

Taking it to the extreme, though (which these folks often neglect to consider), underneath that argument for the "God wants *me* to be happy" pursuit is the fact that one person is above all (me). It's a self-centered, self-absorbed, self, self, self-pursuit—if anyone gets in the way, they'll bounce back, understand, and move on, because we have happiness to pursue.

It's a great sentiment, this happiness above all. And it's made some prosperity gospel folks a lot of money preaching it. One leader said, "No matter what's happening, choose to be happy. Don't focus on what's wrong. Find something positive in your life."[2] That sounds great on the surface, but that kind of blind pursuit of happiness can leave in its wake ruined friendships, families, finances, and plastic surgery nightmares.

Several years ago, I discovered that two close friends were involved in an affair. She was married, with three children. It seemed that I was the last to know what had been happening. What was worse—I'd defended them to other friends when the rumors of their affair started.

"No way," I'd said. "Deena's married. There's no way Rick would sleep with her. I don't believe it. Not them."[3]

So imagine my shock and dismay when over a Chinese dinner of veggie lo mein, using slippery chopsticks, they blurted the news that they'd been having an affair for three months and they loved each other.

I wasn't sure what to say: "Congratulations"? "I'm honored you told me personally"? "I hope you find all the happiness"?

Actually, I didn't say anything. I just sat there. And sat there. All I could think was, *I defended you!*

Finally, Rick shifted uncomfortably in his seat, and Deena's smile faded. "Look," Rick said, "we know what you're going to say."

Now I was intrigued—especially since *I* didn't know what I was going to say. He continued, "Deena's divorcing Dan, and we're getting married."

Still I didn't say anything. My silence forced more tension and they began to defend their actions—even though I'd made no judgments on them or had given any indication I would. They continued to spill the secret. Deena's marriage had been in trouble, and so she'd gone to Rick for comfort—and a few other things.

When I was able to find my voice, I asked, "And the kids? What about them?"

Rick brushed it off. "They'll be fine. You know kids bounce back from these sorts of things."

"Will they. . .be fine? Really? Your mom and dad divorced, Rick. How did that feel for you?"

He harrumphed (such a Prince Charming). "This is about Deena's happiness. Nothing more."

Clearly, I thought. But my big mouth pressed on. "What about the kids' happiness? Don't they deserve to have a mom and dad who at least try to work things out?"

Lots of babbling and bumbling and God wants us to be happy-ing followed.

Toward the end of the conversation, I told them, "Look, you're my friends, and I care deeply about both of you. But you need to know I don't agree with the choices you've made. Those choices to pursue your happiness, while they may feel right to you, carry heavy consequences that will last forever. I just can't be happy for you when I know what you're doing is going to lead to more pain."

I guess I should have felt honored that they still asked me to sing at their wedding.

So Rick and Deena married (sans me as the vocalist) and left a hurricane-size mess in their wake. But at least they're happy. That's what counts, right?

Every once in a while I run into them, and

they tell me how they're doing. It isn't overly awkward; I want the best for them. And I pray that one day they discover the happily ever after that God desires for them. But the saddest thing for me is that I miss them. I miss their friendship—not the tainted friendship I would have now. The old friendship—that had an innocence and truth to it. That part is gone. All because they pursued happiness above all else—because they believed God just wanted them to be happy.

Admittedly, this example is extreme. You may never be involved in an affair or some other such scandalous behavior (I pray you aren't!). It may be the smallest decisions you make to pursue your happiness above all else, because you'll rationalize how much God wants this happiness for you. But the wake of a small self-centered decision is still a wake and can still affect your ability to live happily ever after every day.

CAMP 2: FORGET HAPPINESS. GOD WANTS US TO BE HOLY.

Awhile ago, a book rose to popularity that suggested God's main goal in marriage is not to produce a happy couple but instead to produce a holy couple. Reading the entire book in context, I admit the author makes a great point, and I tend to agree with his arguments (plus I like the author personally). But the trouble with this argument is that too many people hear this message: *God doesn't care about my happiness. In fact, he may not want me to be content at all. It's all and only about pursuing holiness, and I shouldn't give two thoughts to seeking pleasure.*

I've met some of these people; their idea of holiness tends to be drab and humorless. Their faces wear permanent puckered frowns. You've seen them: the ends of their mouths go down and they look as though they haven't seen a smile since Bambi's mother was still living.

I remember once, while working at a magazine for pastors, we received a note from a man who was irked that we incorporated humor in the articles, because "Salvation is no laughing matter. We need to be serious about the things of God." In fact, I knew a woman who used those same words over and over with her family. Whenever she visited, she sucked the joy right out of the room. Her quest for holiness without happiness ended with her family in so much dysfunction, they could have kept a therapist's schedule packed for decades. Although she's now dead, her family still struggles with trying to balance happiness with holiness—as though the two are mutually exclusive.

Isn't it possible that holiness has room to include happiness? That as we pursue holiness we find happiness along the way—if we are open to accepting happiness in different forms? So isn't it okay to ask God to grant us overwhelming happiness in the midst of our characters being formed by holiness? This camp would argue no. I argue otherwise.

Letting Your Life Story Start Over

Forget what has happened in the past for a moment. Forget what just happened five minutes ago, if you have to. Is the happy life, the happily ever after, possible for you starting today and moving forward every day until you reach the forever, heavenly happily ever after? You bet it is. Your life can be better than any Disney story. (And that's no fairy tale. *Ba-dum-dum*.)

I know because I've experienced it. (More on that later.) And I know that the first step is to take stock of how you've been thinking about your daily life. Do you live on either of the above extremes? Or maybe you've tried to pursue happiness and it keeps eluding you. Maybe things have happened *to* you that cause happiness to stay at bay. Or maybe you've done things that cause happiness to keep its distance. It doesn't matter. Now is a new start, a new chapter to your story. And it's the beginning of a great adventure.

I invite you to take this journey with me. In the following chapters we'll look more in depth at what happily ever after really means and how we can arrive there and thrive in it—even if it's happily *even* after.

How much sweeter will our happily ever afters be when we understand our obstacles and we use them instead of allowing them to use us. My first challenge for you (and me) is to take stock of our lives. Is there a part where you've shut out God? Where you've carried expectations that have failed you over and over? Has Prince Charming (in whatever form) failed to arrive? Or has he arrived and he's more like Prince Humperdinck[4]?

Take just five minutes and start to get honest with God and yourself. Tell God you don't trust him, if that's it. Tell him you feel as though he's let you down. That you're just not sure about him or his "plans" for you. Be truthful. Be vulnerable. And then ask him to help you let go of those things you're holding on to, to go out on a limb. Ask him to help you see your life covered by the words *Once upon a time*, with all the anticipation that those words convey. And just see where it takes you.

EMBRACING THE HAPPY LIFE:

- ❧ Who's your favorite fairy-tale character? What is it about that heroine that draws you to her? In what ways does that character exhibit happiness in the midst of unhappy circumstances?

- ❧ In what ways do you wish you were happier? Do you believe the happy life is actually something you can attain? Why or why not?

- ❧ Do you find yourself in either of the camps mentioned in this chapter: the happiness above all or the holiness above all? Are you open to thinking differently about your perspective on happiness?

- ❧ Do you believe that ultimately this life and your happiness is your responsibility, regardless of the circumstances?

WHAT THE BIBLE HAS TO SAY:

"Since [Jesus] himself has gone through suffering and testing, he is able to help us when we are being tested. . . . [He] understands our weaknesses, for he faced all of the same testings we do, yet he did not sin. So let us come boldly to the throne of our gracious God. There we will receive his mercy, and we will find grace to help us when we need it most" (Hebrews 2:18; 4:15–16 NLT).

WHAT'S IN IT FOR ME?

- ✿ Get honest with God and with yourself about your life.

- ✿ Ask God to open your eyes to the possibility of understanding and embracing happiness and holiness in a new way.

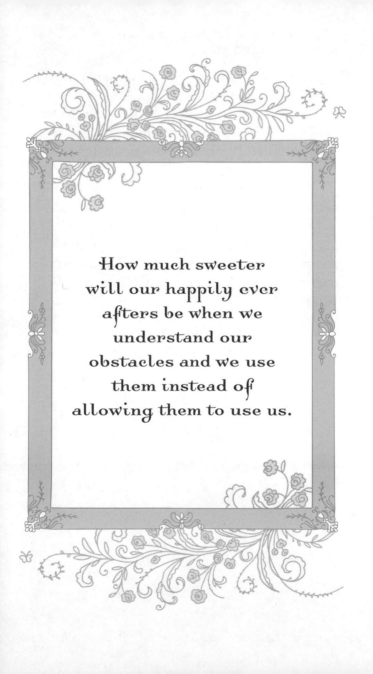

How much sweeter will our happily ever afters be when we understand our obstacles and we use them instead of allowing them to use us.

NOTES: CHAPTER 1

[1] All formerly published by Christianity Today International.

[2] "50 Inspirational Joel Osteen Quotes to Live By," Joel Brown, http://addicted2success.com/quotes/50-inspirational-joel-osteen-quotes-to-live-by/.

[3] Names and some details—except for the slippery chopsticks—have been changed.

[4] From *The Princess Bride*, a delightful fairy-tale movie based on the book of the same name by William Goldman. And it has awesome quotable lines. Watch it or not. "As you wish."

Chapter 2

THE POISONED APPLE. . .
AND OTHER THINGS
THAT GET IN OUR WAY

*Forgetting what is behind and straining
toward what is ahead, I press on toward
the goal to win the prize for which God
has called me heavenward in Christ Jesus.*

PHILIPPIANS 3:13–14 NIV

Poor Snow White. She can't help that she's the fairest in the land, with skin as white as snow, lips as red as blood, and hair as black as ebony. She's simply trying to mind her own business.

But the evil stepmother queen will have none of that. *She* wants to be the fairest and most beautiful in the land, so she sets out to rid the world of Snow White. She orders a huntsman to escort Snow deep into the forest and kill her. As proof of the evil deed, the queen demands that the huntsman return with Snow's heart. But the huntsman is unable to kill the beautiful princess, so he encourages her to flee. Snow lands at a cottage occupied by little-people miners and settles there, caring for the miners as they dance, sing, and whistle while they work.

When the evil queen discovers that Snow White isn't dead—news courtesy of a talking mirror—she becomes enraged and decides to handle the killing task herself. Which goes with the age-old motto: if you want a job done right, do it yourself.

Donning the disguise of an old hag, the queen heads to the seven dwarfs' cottage, where Snow is hiding out, and offers her a delicious, shiny apple to eat. Ah, but the apple is also in disguise. Since Snow apparently was born with beauty but not an overwhelming amount of skeptical prowess, she accepts the apple and bites into it. Immediately Snow falls into a "sleeping death," which can be undone only with "love's first kiss."

The moral of the story here is: never accept unwashed fruit from warty, toothless, unmanicured women. They'll get you every time.

Interestingly enough, in the Brothers Grimm version, the queen tries to kill Snow three times. First, she disguises herself as an old peddler and offers the princess a beautiful lace bodice. The queen laces it so tightly on Snow that the girl faints, and the queen leaves believing she's successfully gotten rid of her competition. The second time, she puts on a new front and offers a comb, which has been poisoned. When the disguised queen brushes Snow's hair, the poison causes Snow again to faint, and again the queen thinks she's succeeded in her mission. But since those no-account dwarfs keep reviving Snow White, the queen tries the third-time's-the-charm approach, poisons an apple, and encourages the simple-minded girl to eat. That does the trick, landing Snow in a glass coffin, until Prince Charming shows up and breaks the spell.

Oh, if only Snow White hadn't been tempted, cajoled, rationalized into nipping a bite of that red delicious. If only she hadn't answered the door and chatted with that troublesome character. *If only*. . .then things might have been different.

Our Poisoned Apples

We all are tempted by and struggle with poisoned apples. Though they may not be literal apples, as our fair princess had, they're just as deadly to our sense of worth, identity, and happiness. They've been known to ruin many a good day, and they hold us back from becoming who God has purposed us to be. These apples come in many different varieties. Let's look at the four biggies.

POISONED APPLE #1: STUFF THAT ISN'T SIN BUT ISN'T IN OUR BEST INTEREST.

This is the type of apple Snow held on to. By accepting the gifts, she wasn't doing anything wrong, but she certainly wasn't discerning that these "well-meaning" folks delivering items she didn't order might put her in danger. How often do we find ourselves in similar situations with these apples?

My friend Jana[1] works for a company that has essentially sucked her soul dry. A gifted designer, she remains in her position because she doesn't believe she'd be able to find anything else that would allow her to use her gifts. "The company pushes the agenda that I can't survive without them, and I've begun to believe them," she admitted to me one day over lunch.

About a year ago, as more and more layoffs happened at her company, she informed me that she was going to start looking for another job. "I have a six-year plan. If the company lasts and I can survive the layoffs, then I'm getting out of there."

"Um, six years?" I asked, trying nonchalantly to lift my jaw off the pile of french fries in front of me.

I love my friend. She's a super-gifted woman who is super unhappy. Is staying in her morale-busting job a sin? Not necessarily. But I daresay having a six-year exit strategy is probably not in her best interest. And each time I see her, she's more unhappy, more unhealthy, and more unsure of the talents she possesses.

I know another woman, Robin,[2] who is beautiful. As in so gorgeous you want to hate her just because. She also happens to be really sweet, so that doubles the hate factor. But then, because she's so sweet, you just *can't* hate her—which makes you feel guilty because you want to and don't want to all at the same time. But Robin makes terrible decisions about men. She dates duds—usually the ones who are only too happy to allow her to help them financially. They also talk down to her, insult her, and disrespect her.

When I've asked why she allows this treatment, she shrugs and confesses that those are the only guys who ask her out. She doesn't see herself as the beautiful, kind woman God created.

Is it sinful for her to date those guys? No, but those guys certainly aren't in her best interest and they're never going to help her see her true value—or help her get ahead financially.

While we may not struggle with the above issues, I daresay most of us do struggle with another kind of poisoned apple in the same category: distractions. These little babies hold us off from pursuing our best (and often we pursue the distractions believing those will actually bring us real and lasting happiness). They're the smaller stuff, or what I like to call poisoned prunes. They keep us regular. . .*ly* held up from doing the stuff we need to do to pursue true happiness. Television, video games, shopping, comfort/stress eating, social media. I've known many people who camp out on Facebook, Twitter, Pinterest, and Instagram. One friend admitted jokingly that his wife calls

Twitter his mistress because he spends so much time on it.

Many years ago, *Leadership Journal* ran a cartoon of Martin Luther sitting in front of a television set, holding a remote control and channel surfing. The title offered the comment, "If there had been television in 1517," and the punch line was Luther saying, "I ought to write down those 95 things I was thinking about the other day. . .nyaaah. . .let's see what's on the tube."[3]

The great reformer, who wrote ninety-five charges against the Catholic church and ended up changing the landscape of Christianity by introducing Protestantism, was procrastinating so that he could watch a little more TV.

In the end, these distractions are empty, time-wasting, happiness-busting bunk. I may enjoy it for the moment, but when I think of all the other things I can accomplish today that can bring real, lasting happiness, I feel a little ill over my stupid choices. How much weight could I have lost had I decided to go outside and take a walk rather than channel surf for two hours and ultimately land on a whole bunch of nothing? How much personal face-to-face time could I have had with my family and friends had I not spent hours on Facebook—often while sitting next to one of them!—seeing what great things everyone else has accomplished and realizing that I'm truly a dud in the professional, domestic, and relational departments.

I'm talking to myself here. I waste time on distractions. Just writing this section I checked my e-mail twelve times. I walked into the kitchen and got something to drink. I petted the dog. I thought about putting a load of laundry in the washer. I flipped through the most recent issue of *Real Simple*. I wrote out a grocery list. I went to the bathroom. I organized my fingernail polish bottles. I checked Facebook. I stared out the window. I checked my e-mail again.

None of those things is sinful. But when I'm under a deadline and procrastinating, they aren't in my best interest and stifle the happiness I could have enjoyed over a job well done—even if I did discover that bottle of cotton candy-pink polish I'd forgotten I had.

POISONED APPLE #2: WHAT WE'VE DONE IN THE PAST THAT HOLDS US FROM BEING FREE TODAY.

Full disclosure: I struggle a lot with this poisoned apple. I was raised in a church tradition that held holiness in high regard, for which I'm grateful. Unfortunately, holiness was often defined as a list of rules. If you did this, you got holy points and were a good Christian.

If you did this other thing, though, boy oh boy, you better repent quick because God might withhold his love and blessing from you and instead rain down punishment. It seemed as though all I ever did was repent! I saw God as this Creator who "loved" us unconditionally—because that's what we sang about in Sunday school—but really, he eagerly watched and waited for me to mess up so that he could judge and punish me. It was a fear-based religion for me, and it kept me bound and unhappy for years.

I didn't smoke, I didn't drink, I didn't sleep around. All pluses in the church's list of rules, so I could feel pretty good about myself with that, which only set the stage for me to begin to feel superior (not listed as a negative in the rules). Add to that the fact that I was an entitled, spoiled, only-child brat—an unfortunate and painful combination—and my family, friends, classmates, and church community had a real winner on their hands. My adolescence and young adult years were a great breeding ground for me to become an angry, bitter, critical, judgmental, often-nasty person. (I hear my mother saying amen.) And of course, I'm a Gen Xer, so I was really in great shape.[4]

I pushed others, because as hard as I tried, I just couldn't live up to what I believed

God expected of me: to be perfect. And so in some sense, in order to displace my own shortcomings and severe insecurities in the "goodness" department, I turned the scale on others, expecting them to be perfect, too. I didn't believe God's grace really covered me, so I didn't extend grace to others. To quote a great line from the movie *Old Fashioned*:[5] I was using grace as a "brick wall." The bar was set impossibly high, and I became judge and jury. I cringe even writing this paragraph. My past brings intense shame, regret, and angst at how truly stupid and wrong I was.

A few years ago, someone on Facebook posted: "What do you regret most: the things you've said or the things that you haven't said?" A majority of the responses were regret for the things that should have been said but weren't. I've felt the most regret over the things that I've said that I shouldn't have.

The truth is that I hurt people. And I abhor that about my past and myself. And at times—especially when I'm feeling low—a memory will float back into my mind of something I said or did that caused pain and displayed my dark side. And right after that, a thought will come, *You're such a terrible person. Look at how bad you are. You don't deserve God's grace. You don't deserve to be happy*. Those memories and damning thoughts can hold me captive and can shove me into a deep pit of despair.

But I'm not alone. In my work I meet a lot of people and I enjoy hearing their stories and dreams. It helps me understand where they've come from and where they hope to go. I discover how God has woven his image all through them. And it connects me with them because I know a bit more about them. And I can tell you that every person I've ever met has regrets. She's done something or made choices that turned out to be wrong for her. It doesn't matter how put together a person appears on the outside, how famous or anonymous she is, deep down she wrestles with shame of some sort.

I've met wonderful women who have struggled because they had abortions, broke up with or cheated on the guy who really was "Mr. Perfect," betrayed a friend, quit a team or job because it was too difficult or demanding, married Mr. Wrong, accused a relative of something that turned out to be untrue, lied to get a promotion or to get ahead of a friend or coworker, and the list goes on and on. They've felt deep remorse and have sought forgiveness, yet the regret continues to cling to them like a parasite. And just when these women try to move ahead into grasping their beautiful worth and purpose, the past comes storming back into their minds, accusing, judging, and sentencing them to a lifetime of disgrace.

POISONED APPLE #3: WHAT OTHERS HAVE
DONE TO US THAT KEEPS US FROM BEING
FREE TODAY.

Sharon[6] is from one of the most dysfunctional families I've ever met. While she was
growing up, she was sexually, physically, emotionally, psychologically, and spiritually abused.
She was force-fed religion by parents who
never told her they loved her. More than forty
years later, and now with deceased parents,
Sharon still struggles with the pain, anger,
bitterness, and betrayal that her mom and dad
brought into her life.

She is one of the most hopeless people
I know. Every time I see her, she shares how
unhappy she is. Not only that, but her health
is a mess. She has absolutely every right to be
angry over what happened to her. The more
I hear about her childhood, the more angry I
become—and I wasn't even there. Holding on to
that anger like a lover, though, has brought its
own misfortune beyond what happened in her
past. She's cleaved to the past, and by doing
so, she has created a monster that has taken
over her present and brought on its own pain:
her husband has cheated on her, her children
are estranged from her, she suffers major
health issues, and she refuses to reconnect

with God. And as long as she continues to cling to the past hurts and betrayals, she will never know real restoration; she will never discover her real identity and value in Christ. She will never experience the happily-ever-after life that she was meant to know.

I know people who have suffered terrible things at the hands of others. I've talked with women who were abducted, raped, beaten, strangled, abused, sold into human trafficking, forced to do unthinkable acts. They've survived, but some of them have held on to the pain of the past in such a way that it has changed them. It has scarred them beyond how others scarred them. Instead of breaking the curse placed on them, they've sewn it on their own shoulders and determined to keep it alive and well.

POISONED APPLE #4: OUR WRONG CHOICES, OR WHAT THE BIBLE CALLS SIN.

This is different from choices of the past. This apple is very present: it's about the choices we make today—the ones that clearly hurt others and ourselves. They are a clear rebellion against God. We often mistakenly think of ourselves a little better if we aren't doing the "big" sins: committing adultery, murdering someone, beating our cats, robbing a convenience store, listening incessantly to the

Beatles' "Yellow Submarine."

I find the sins I struggle with most, however, are more along insipid lines—those sneaky little devils that I can rationalize and justify: judgmentalism, misplaced expectations, pride, white lies, lustful thoughts. Mostly, they're attitude issues. When I was in college I read a book by Tony Campolo in which he claimed that sin is anything that dehumanizes someone. That stuck with me—mostly because I thought, *Yowsa, I do that all the time!* When I judge someone, I make them a little less than me, because I set myself up to be better: I know better, I act better, I speak better (I dehumanize them). When I fantasize about some hot guy, I make him into the image I want him to be (I dehumanize him). When I spit out a little white lie that really would never hurt anybody or manipulate someone to get what I want, I treat another person with the idea that I can deceive them—and they'll be deceived because, really, they aren't smart enough to know that I'm not telling the truth or that I'm manipulating them (I dehumanize them). Dehumanizing someone is a sin because we strip them of their dignity of being made in God's image. So it doesn't matter that we don't literally murder someone. We can cut them up really well in our minds. We can manipulate and force our expectations on another person to be and do what we want. We are experts at dehumanizing others. Sin is ugly, my friend. And when we bite into that poisoned apple, it can wreak all kinds of havoc on our peace and happiness.

Ditching the Poisoned Apples

An interesting part of the Brothers Grimm version of *Snow White* is that after being tricked twice (the lacy bodice and the poisoned comb), when an old farmer's wife (the disguised evil queen) displays an apple, Snow isn't eager to pursue the tasting. She must have had a moment in which she thought, *The last two presents made me faint. Perhaps this is a trick and I should avoid the apple*. Way to go, Snow.

Sensing Snow White's reluctance, the disguised queen cuts the apple in half and eats the white half, which is harmless. Snow White falls for the hoax and eagerly bites into the crunchiest, juiciest, deadliest apple she's ever eaten. Unfortunately, it's also the half that is poisoned. Oh no, Snow.

We need to do something about the poisoned apples that hold us back from experiencing the happy life, the life that God has designed especially for us. But what?

Here's what the writer of Hebrews says we should do:

> *Let us also lay aside every weight, and sin which clings so closely, and let us run with endurance the race that is set before us, looking to Jesus, the founder and perfecter of our faith, who for the joy that was set before him endured the cross, despising the shame, and is seated at the right hand of the throne of God.*
> HEBREWS 12:1–2 ESV

Sounds simple, doesn't it? Essentially, the writer tells us to get rid of *anything* that weighs us down, that "slows us down or holds us back" (TLB), that "hinders" us from pursuing the race that is specifically designed for us. Obviously, we repent of any wrongdoing that we have committed or continue to commit. Those things so easily entangle us on our journey. But more often, it's the pesky distractions. Even good things can hinder us from living to our fullest potential. How many times have we been slowed down over worries, interests, or entertainments? They aren't bad in and of themselves, but if they sidetrack us from living out the happily ever after God intended, then they aren't worth giving attention to.

Sometimes I can get frustrated when someone tells me to "just do" something, as if it's that simple. I almost popped a family member one time when he lost an insane amount of weight and then smugly told me that if I want to lose the pounds, I should simply stop eating and start exercising.

Seriously? I hadn't figured out that one, so thanks for the unsolicited input. (I didn't physically hurt him, although I did wonder if knocking him on his rump would constitute my daily workout.) As much as I hated hearing him assert that bit of wisdom, the reality is that he is right. Do I want to lose weight? Then I have to stop noshing on Ben & Jerry's at midnight, pull out some carrots, and take a walk. It *is* that simple.

Ah, but is it really? If it were, wouldn't I already be a size 2? Wouldn't I be sinless? Wouldn't Candy Crush or Spider Solitaire never tempt me? Wouldn't I burst out in song, while walking with cute little raccoons and squirrels humming beside me?

When I'm going along well in my journey, that's usually when the antagonist in my life story brings up my past and encourages me to obsess about it, that I'm no different today from what I was—I'm still a sinner. If I let it, the temptation to believe that weighs me down and keeps me from enduring my race toward joy.

So it really *isn't* that simple.

How do we stay focused? How do we get rid of the apple? How do we endure?

By following the advice of the author of Hebrews: fix our eyes on Jesus, the "founder and perfecter" of our faith. Jesus ran the race before us, so he knows what we will encounter. And best yet, he ran it knowing that joy was set before him. Not the joy that he would have by returning to heaven. He was assured the joy of knowing that through him, we also can experience joy. When I look to Jesus, and laser my focus on him, I no longer *want* to act as if I'm the only perfect one or think that I'm the only *imperfect* one. Hallelujah, and pass the banana bread.

The writer of Hebrews illustrates our life stories as a race. And a race is a journey. We continually have to gauge our pace, our partners, our self-talk, our hydration. We run to win—but winning is work. Running is difficult enough when we're in the right shape and wearing the right clothes. But if we've packed on a few pounds and we're wearing sweat pants and a parka, we aren't going to get too far. So we ditch the things that keep us from running well on the path—and I know we all know what those things are for each of us.

Your distractions and weaknesses aren't the same as mine, but when we get honest with ourselves, we know the things we struggle with. I can count out at least five of my hindrances before you finish reading this sentence. I bet you can do the same about your hindrances. *Those* are the things we need to diligently get rid of—and we need to persevere at it or "run with endurance."

Don't quit. Don't get frustrated because it's too difficult. Keep running—even when you don't want to. Because your race is specific *to you*. God has designed your race track to be filled with wonder and challenge. And it is yours and yours alone. If you quit, if you get distracted, if you allow the hardships to slow you down, if you persist in rebelling against what God says is good for you, you miss the joy of the journey.

Consider Me Your Friendly Neighborhood Dwarf

Snow White was one fortunate broad. Every time she passed out, the dwarfs arrived home, evaluated the situation, and offered life-saving aid (except for the last time when they stuffed her in a glass coffin and waited until the prince showed up—but we'll discuss that later). So while I may not be a bearded miner named Happy, at five foot four I'm short enough to set my allegiance with this band of whistling fiends and offer some practical help for how to ditch and be on the lookout for poisoned apples. And most of it comes directly from scripture.

1. REMEMBER WHO YOU REALLY ARE.

You aren't your past. You aren't what others teased or accused. You aren't what you too often may believe when you look in the mirror. This is who you really are: a new person in Christ. "If anyone is in Christ, he is a new creation; old things have passed away; behold, all things have become new" (2 Corinthians 5:17 NKJV).

I know a woman who is delightful to be around. She's so friendly and funny. I love spending time with her. She can tell the best stories, and she always has me laughing. People flock to her. They love being around her. She's just one of the coolest people I know. But she doesn't believe it when I tell her that. One day she confessed the reason was that her mother always called her "a lazy, no good, stupid girl." This woman carried those lies into her adult life. She would "get rid" of them, as Hebrews tells us, but the words would sneak back into her mind and haunt her. So she began to rewrite the words and quote Scripture to herself. She claims Christ as her own; therefore she is a new creation. She is created in God's image (and he's no slouch). It's taken a lot of new self-talk, of reminding herself constantly of how God views her, but as she clutches the truth of who she really is, her mother's voice has become more faint.

I'm so grateful that I'm no longer who I was. I would be hopeless if I were. But thanks to the God who created me and purposed me to show off the beauty of Jesus, I am a new creation—one whom he is shaping and polishing every day—and will continue to do so until the moment I take my last breath. And he's doing the same with you.

2. REMEMBER THAT YOUR PAST IS RIGHT WHERE IT SHOULD BE: IN THE PAST.

My husband was married before. It was a difficult marriage filled with betrayal and heartache. He was so wounded from that relationship that it took him years to be restored. So when we got married, we put one scripture in our wedding program that would become our marriage motto:

"Forget the former things; do not

*dwell on the past. See, I am doing a
new thing! Now it springs up; do you
not perceive it? I am making a way
in the wilderness and streams in the
wasteland."*
Isaiah 43:18-19 NIV

Every time I read that verse, I have to stop and catch my breath. It puts me in such awe—not only that God *can* do that, but that he *wants* to do it. Such amazing grace he offers us. And he continues his work with us—"I *am making* a way." He doesn't say, "I made a way." He lets us know that his work to bring us into new places of joy and peace isn't ending.

When we fall short of God's perfect standard for us and we seek his forgiveness, we get a double blessing: we receive his forgiveness *and* his forgetfulness. King David tells us that "as far as the east is from the west, so far does [God] remove our transgressions from us" (Psalm 103:12 ESV). So why should we allow the pain of our mess-ups to dog us when God doesn't even remember them? The evil one whispers in our ear, *Remember you're a failure.* And you go to God and say, "But I'm such a failure. Remember that thing I did?" And God responds, "What thing? I don't remember any 'thing.'"

So if God, through his mercy, doesn't hold

our past against us and desires for us to keep focused on Jesus, with our eyes straight ahead, then why do we add a handicap to ourselves, which slows us down and keeps us from our happiness, by bringing it up?

One of my favorite verses has saved me from despair more times than I can count, as the cliché goes:

> *Not that I have already obtained all this, or have already arrived at my goal, but I press on to take hold of that for which Christ Jesus took hold of me. Brothers and sisters, I do not consider myself yet to have taken hold of it. But one thing I do:* **Forgetting what is behind** *and straining toward what is ahead, I press on toward the goal to win the prize for which God has called me heavenward in Christ Jesus.*
> Philippians 3:12–14 niv, emphasis added

We have biblical permission to forget the past. We can forget our past wrongdoings and mistakes. But we must also forget the past things done against us. Until we deal with the root of those things and then let them go, they have the potential to continue to poison us. They poison our perspective, our attitude, our thinking, our ability to love and be loved, to recognize and embrace happiness. Let me be clear: we don't forget because they mean nothing. We don't forget and then allow something bad to happen to us in a repeating fashion. We don't forget, in that we learn from what has happened to us and we pursue the part of it that will make us stronger and wiser. But ultimately we choose to forget (let it and its power to restrain go) because God (the ultimate judge) has promised to avenge the hurts that we've suffered. So we *have* to let go in order to reach for the true prize: our happily ever after—the one here today and the eternal one.[7]

3. REMEMBER THAT YOU ACTUALLY CONTROL YOUR HAPPINESS.

The truth is that you determine how happy you will be. Nobody else controls that. Not your mother. Not your dad. Not your significant other. Not your kids or kinsmen. Not your boss or friends. Not the president or the governor or the mayor or the clerk at Macy's who gave you an extra discount on that lovely little black dress you'd been eyeing. You alone determine your level of happiness.

Last year I watched two elderly Christian women face the dire diagnosis of cancer. Both opted not to pursue treatment options. One was miserable through the entire journey. She questioned God over why this thing had to happen to her. She rebuffed her children's well-meaning attempts at finding joy in the midst of the darkness. She complained. She melodramatically suffered. In short, she was unhappy. She could not be comforted, and she experienced terrible bouts of paralyzing fear.

The other woman, however, experienced intense pain as her body shut down. But she kept her eyes focused on how she could continue to help others for Christ's kingdom. She sewed dresses to send to children in South America. She even asked her son to hold her up to the quilting loom so she could complete blankets for the "less fortunate." She was quick to smile and thank those who cared for her. Her companion was gratitude. She chose happiness. And her reward was peace, joy, and comfort.

Both women experienced real pain and suffering. One chose happiness; the other didn't. Watching these two women, I knew clearly what I wanted to choose if I ever found myself in a similar situation. I may not be able to control what happens to me, but I can control how I respond to it.

The apostle Paul gives us great advice on this topic:

Rejoice in the Lord always. I will say it again: Rejoice! . . . . Whatever is true,

whatever is noble, whatever is right,
whatever is pure, whatever is lovely,
*whatever is admirable—if **anything** is*
excellent or praiseworthy—think about
such things. . . . And the God of peace
will be with you.
PHILIPPIANS 4:4, 8–9 NIV, emphasis added

I wish I could tell you that I no longer struggle with tempting poisoned apples, that I'm way beyond that. But you and I both know that would be disingenuous of me. When we share our weakness (see James 5:16), it's trickier for us to cling to sin and carry the weight that holds us back and keeps us unhappy and unhealthy. I've found that in the moments when I'm weakest and tempted to move my focus from joy to my circumstances, then if I quote that passage and mean it and begin to count my blessings—even the most mundane, ordinary ones—my right focus returns. The Lord gifts me with peace. And as those weak moments re-present themselves, I share my struggles with others whom I trust, so they can pray for me, and so that restoration and real healing happens.

When the Prince Arrives

The third time may have been the charm for the evil queen, but it certainly wasn't for Snow White. After eating the apple, she fell into a "sleeping death," which could be broken only by "love's first kiss." Before this, the dwarfs had always been able to evaluate the situation and figure out the root problem and then revive Snow White. But this time, they were unable to determine what had caused Snow to fall under the curse. So they did what any normal person would do: they stuffed her into a glass coffin. (Am I the only one who finds that slightly odd and creepy?) But glory hallelujah, the prince arrived and revived our princess once and for all. He redeemed and restored what the poisoned apple had taken from Snow.

If Snow White hadn't eaten the apple, she'd probably be an old maid (literally), still living and hanging out with the dwarfs in the forest. But instead, that bite was redeemed and she met someone who restored her to what she was meant to be—the fairest queen in the land. It's as if the Brothers Grimm plagiarized the idea from the apostle Paul, who wrote: "We know that all things work together for good to those who love God, to those who are the called according to His purpose" (Romans 8:28 NKJV).

Jesus does that for us. He takes what we could never imagine being redeemable and he works his spiritual magic onto it, reconciling and restoring, allowing us to grow stronger and wiser and to find joy even in the mistakes of eating poisoned apples.

EMBRACING THE HAPPY LIFE:

❀ What type of poisoned apple are you most tempted to bite into?

❀ What are some ways you can be more alert and aware of the apples that present themselves to you?

WHAT THE BIBLE HAS TO SAY:

"Now that we know what we have—Jesus, this great High Priest with ready access to God—let's not let it slip through our fingers. We don't have a priest who is out of touch with our reality. He's been through weakness and testing, experienced it all—all but the sin. So let's walk right up to him and get what he is so ready to give. Take the mercy, accept the help" (Hebrews 4:15–16 MSG).

WHAT'S IN IT FOR ME?

❀ Find a mentor or close friend who will help you steer clear of poisoned apples. Ask that person to hold you accountable and to remind you of your calling and worth. Give her permission to call you out—especially if you're biting off an apple that leads to sin.

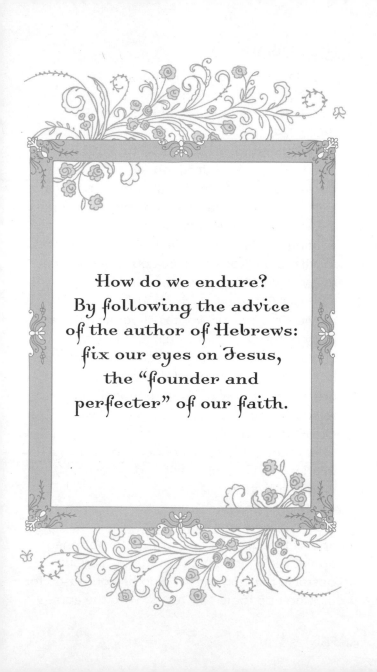

How do we endure?
By following the advice
of the author of Hebrews:
fix our eyes on Jesus,
the "founder and
perfecter" of our faith.

NOTES: CHAPTER 2

[1] Name has been changed.

[2] Name has been changed.

[3] Ed Koehler, *Leadership Journal* (Spring 1988), 124.

[4] Generation X (born 1965 to 1980) is said to be the skeptical, sarcastic, hopeless generation. Although, I really do like being a Gen Xer. We're a humorous bunch. For more info on how the generations view God and religion differently and what difference that makes to our society, check out *Generational IQ* by Haydn Shaw and yours truly.

[5] *Old Fashioned* is a seriously great indie movie. One of my favorites. If you can get a copy of the DVD and watch it, you'll laugh, cry, and be seriously romanticized. The companion book *The Old Fashioned Way* also gives a great look at how to live intentionally in our relationships. Full disclosure: yeah, I wrote *The Old Fashioned Way*—but even still, I think it offers thought-provoking ideas to take your relationships in a different and refreshingly unique direction.

[6] Name has been changed.

[7] While we make light of the poisoned apples by spotlighting a fairy tale, poisoned apples really are a huge—and very serious—obstacle to living the life God has purposed for us. Don't be fooled by toying with the apples

because they're intriguing or because you think you can handle them. Dealing with some of these apples—especially the ones in which someone else has deeply hurt you—are beyond the scope of this book. There are hundreds of excellent resources that can take you through the next step(s) to ditching those poisoned apples. I am not an expert in that area—nor do I claim to be. I'm a fellow journeyman. This book is a first step—or a fortieth first step, if that's the case. Please surround yourself with great dwarfs who can hold you accountable and help prop you up when you're tempted to take a teeny, tiny little bite. I encourage you to get the help and the accountability that you need.

Chapter 3

DEALING WITH THE UGLY STEPSISTERS. . .OR THOSE ANNOYING DWARFS. TAKE YOUR PICK

*We can say with confidence,
"The Lord is my helper, so I will have no
fear. What can mere people do to me?"*
HEBREWS 13:6 NLT

stopped by the grocery store a few weeks ago to pick up items for supper. It had been a good day. I'd been productive at work. Traffic on the way home had moved quickly and I'd caught most of the green lights. Even my grocery store experience was pleasant. No one bumped me with a cart or pushed me out of the way to snatch the tomato I'd been eyeing. My step was light. All was well. I took my place in the checkout line. Three people were ahead of me—all with fewer than ten items.

Yep, this is my day, I thought and smiled, mentally shuffling through my to-do list for the evening. Out of the corner of my eye, I caught the cashier's frown. Then bits of her words drifted back to me.

"Well, if you hadn't forgotten it, I wouldn't have to walk all the way over to the customer service counter for you."

The female customer, looking frazzled, apologized and tried to smile.

The two men standing behind her both grunted impatiently as we all watched the cashier stomp off toward the service desk. I just shrugged. I wasn't completely sure what the commotion was about, but I was having a good day. No big deal.

The woman apologized to everybody in line. "I'm really sorry. I wasn't thinking. It's been a crazy day."

The two men grunted again, grabbed their items, and stormed off in search of another line. I glanced at the other checkouts. Ours was the shortest, so I wasn't sure where they were going. But I shrugged again.

Look at my good fortune, I thought. *I just jumped up to next in line. Excellent!*

The woman again apologized. I felt sorry for her since she'd caused such a "huge" holdup.

She must have bad credit or maybe she tried to return something half-eaten. "What happened?" I asked.

"I forgot my frequent shopper's savings card."

I blinked. *That's it?* I half laughed. *That's nothing! I do that all the time.*

"You can use mine," I offered—not that it mattered, since the cashier had already left.

"I tried to borrow the last guy's." She nodded toward where the other customers had stood. "The cashier said she wasn't allowed to use anybody else's or she'd get fired."

Fired? That seemed melodramatic.

Before I could say anything, the cashier returned, looking as if she'd stopped by the produce section to lick a turnip. She punched some numbers into the system and rang up the woman's items, never once glancing at her.

Instead, she turned toward me and smiled like a Cheshire cat.

"Hello," she said pointedly and over-politely. "I'm sorry for making you wait."

Uh-oh. I'd been caught in the middle of these situations before. Not interested. I was having a good day.

The cashier proceeded to tell me hello again and apologize. Another three times. Okay, point taken.

"Not a big deal," I said. "I waited, what, an extra two minutes? Seriously. I would have waited that long if the other two customers had stayed in line."

The cashier finished with the customer— still not saying a word to her—then turned her attention on me. I thrust my store savings card at her.

Please don't yell at me, I mentally pled. *I'm having a good day. I just want to purchase my stuff and go home.*

But it wasn't meant to be. Instead, she launched into a tirade about "stupid people not bringing their savings cards and how difficult is it really to remember the card when you know you're going to be at the grocery store and why didn't she just leave it in her purse it's not like she never goes to the grocery store and now I had to walk all the way"—twenty feet—"over to the service counter and I've been here five hours and haven't gotten a break and I'm tired of people who can't even remember something as simple as a card and I'm sorry you had to wait. *Hello*," she said to the person behind me without taking a break in her rant. "I'm so sorry you've had to wait. You do have your savings card, right?"

Oh, please, God, let that person have his savings card.

I *had* been having a good day. Then I met Ms. Cranky Pants, who threatened to destroy it. She annoyed me. And since she was bigger than me, she also scared me a little. Fortunately, I think I could have outrun her if I needed to (she'd been on her feet for five hours, after all).

Her attitude and behavior were inappropriate. She took them both out on an unsuspecting customer, and I could have been next. Fortunately, I was able to take my items, exit the store, and leave her far, far behind.

But what about those Mr. and Ms. Cranky Pants whom you can't outrun or leave in a grocery store?

My friend Dawn just shakes her head as she says, "*People.* You know, there's only one thing that keeps me from being a really amazing Christian. Other people."

As we travel through life, we often run across obstacles that get in our way of being the best doggone Christian women we can be: many of those obstacles are called *people*.

Several years ago, I read actor Charles Grodin's autobiography, which is simply titled *It Would Be So Nice If You Weren't Here*. That's the story of my life too many times! Can I get an amen?

Thorny people, I call them. They show up in our lives and cause us all kinds of untold frustration. I've had people enter my life who had the uncanny ability to find my last nerve and tap dance all over it. Sometimes they're family members. Sometimes they're neighbors. Coworkers. Grocery store cashiers. But they're there and they seem to have been tasked with making our lives miserable.

Cinderella had those dreadful stepsisters and stepmother to deal with.

Belle had Gaston.

Snow White had the witch. *And* those seven little men always under her feet, getting in her way, constantly whistling, while she cleaned, cooked, and mothered them.

Nobody ever talks about the problems with the seven dwarfs. But we can break down those dwarfs into people who challenge our sainthood and sanity.

The Seven Pains in the Neck

When Walt Disney created the seven dwarfs, he wanted them to be recognizable as "regular guys," people we could identify from our neighborhoods. And while underneath all those quirky exteriors lie kindhearted and sweet characters, on the surface they can drive a person crazy.

Consider them:[1]

First there's Doc, a.k.a. Mr. Know-It-All. He's the leader of the group. You've met these self-identified Einsteins. It doesn't matter what is happening, they have an opinion, an answer, or advice, and they aren't afraid to offer it—loud and often. Even when they're clearly out of their league or wrong, they still want to impress you with their stunning amount of knowledge.

Next we have Bashful. Cute blushes, but really: grow a spine already and stick up for yourself. These are overwhelmingly self-conscious people, to the point that you can't have an in-depth conversation with them without them becoming uncomfortable, giggly, or doing something else nonsensical. It's like pulling a baby seal out of a pinhole in the ice.

It's doable but breathtakingly exhausting.

Grumpy is our next fun-loving individual. He can take a sunny day and yank the sunlight right out of it. It doesn't matter what it is, this person sucks the joy from *everything*: Christianity, holidays, birthdays, double rainbows, long-eared clumsy puppies, unicorns, and Baskin Robbins chocolate peanut butter ice cream on a sugar cone.

Sneezy, a.k.a. Mr. Hypochondriac. Or Mr. I'll-Share-My-Sickness-with-You-All. Or Mr. I-Need-to-Learn-Manners. Sneezy never covers his mouth when he sneezes, have you noticed that? He probably doesn't wash his hands afterward either. (Maybe that's why Grumpy is the way he is.) Have you met these people? Something is always wrong with them. And usually they're only too glad to share all the details about it. And I do mean all.

Dopey is next. I prefer to think of him as Can You Use Your Brain to Figure This Thing Out—Why Do I Always Have to Be Bothered with It? These people aren't stupid; they're in la la land. Bless their hearts. Dopey couldn't even get it together enough to speak. If I were cruel, I'd call him blond. But then, wait a sec, *I'm* blond. . . .

Number six on our dwarfy countdown is Sleepy. He never wants to do anything fun because he's always too tired. He goes to bed at nine sharp and won't budge from his schedule. He yawns loudly—and it's usually during a really important part in a movie that, of course, you miss.

And finally there's Happy. How can Happy be irritating, you say? This person is overly optimistic to the point of causing nausea. His female counterpart is known as Pollyanna or Little Mary Sunshine. This fellow can always find something way too positive in the midst of stress. Lose a finger? No problem, you still have nine others. These folks also tend to be morning people and gravitate irritatingly toward night owls. They ooh and aah at sunrises and want to actually get up early to—get this—enjoy the day. It's just wrong.[2]

A rabbit trail here. One year I went to Disneyland and bought two T-shirts that I thought were hilarious. One had a picture of Dopey on it with a big arrow pointing to the side. It said, "I'm with Grumpy." The other shirt had a picture of Grumpy on it with a big arrow pointing to the other side. It said, "I'm with Dopey." I thought these would be fun for my husband and me to wear. He didn't agree. Guess which of the shirts I thought would work best for him?

The seven dwarfs really aren't bad people. Annoying sometimes, but they don't cause you to lose your joy. That's how many people in our lives are. They cause just minor irritations. No big deal. You can slough it off. Snow White clearly did. They may tend to bother you most when you've had a really bad day, are sick, or stressed, and then you might snap, but the feeling goes away. It's quickly forgotten. Kids, spouses, moms, and friends usually fall into these categories.

But what about those people who enter your life and they're not just minor irritations? You know the ones—they can easily turn your focus off your spiritual endurance, your happily ever after, and make you want to take them down with an elephant tranquilizer gun. They're joy-less, mean, spiteful, hard to work with, bossy, pushy, manipulative, critical, negative. In short, they feel toxic. Whenever you're around them, you tighten up, knowing something is going to happen. These are the people you don't have feelings *for*, you have feelings *about*.

During one harsh season that lasted about five years, I dealt daily with a number of toxic people. Weeks went by during which I went home every night, threw myself on the couch, and sobbed. It became so bad that I suffered with migraines, ground my teeth at night to the point that I chipped a front tooth, gained sixty pounds, and barked angrily at all the people I loved deeply. Several close friends told me they worried about my stress level. It would be an understatement to say I was miserable. Imagine getting your arm stuck in a toilet trying to retrieve your cell phone. Yeah, it was even worse than *that*.

The fortunate part with my experience (and I expect with yours) is that you and I probably don't deal with the level of toxic folks that our fairy-tale princesses had to suffer. Rapunzel's "mother" literally locked Rapunzel in a tower. Ursula stole Ariel's voice. Sleeping Beauty and Snow White were poisoned. Cinderella was enslaved. All thanks to toxic people.

While my strained season was wretched and long, I learned some important things about myself, my faith, and the Thorny Ones. The writer of Hebrews offers an interesting take on these toxic folks.

> *Let us fix our eyes on Jesus, the author and perfecter of our faith, who for the joy set before him endured the cross, scorning its shame, and sat down at the right hand of the throne of God.* **Consider him who endured such opposition from sinful men, so that you will not grow weary and lose heart.**
> HEBREWS 12:2–3 NIV 1984, emphasis added

I love verse 3. Basically it says, *Don't get discouraged. Think about Jesus and what he had to deal with from nasty people—how they treated him and insulted him and plotted against him. His experiences were way harsher than yours. But he pushed on because of the goal. And you can, too, with his help. So let that encourage you to keep on keeping on.*

It makes me almost not mind having toxic people in my life. Almost.

Try Not to Take Things Personally

Here's the truth: it really isn't about you or me. We heap more trouble, frustration, and stress on ourselves when we make those dire, difficult situations about us. It's easy to do, of course. It certainly feels personal when the witch goes after Snow White. It feels personal when Cinderella's malicious step-relations treat her like a maid. It feels personal when someone steals our ideas and uses them against us. It feels personal when who we thought was Prince Charming dumps us because "I'm not in love with you." It feels utterly, unreservedly, absolutely, unequivocally personal.

Although it may *feel* that way, it's important to remember that feelings and actuality aren't always the same things. We feel that those things were directed against us personally because we're viewing them from our own storybook points of view. Which means they're subjective, biased.

My mom likes to remind me that most people are self-centered so they aren't thinking about me when something happens. They're more focused on themselves.

Look at the Pharisees who were constantly bothering Jesus. Why? Because Jesus was holding a mirror to their own sinfulness. They felt he was "making" them look bad. It wasn't about Jesus as much as it was about them, *their* way of life, *their* issues, *their* traditions, *their* power. Jesus knew that—and he didn't allow them to take his eyes off his goals, his joy, his strength. And that's what he calls us to do, as we follow his example.

My friend Deborah[3] acted horribly toward me when I got engaged. She fought me on every decision I made. She uttered harsh comments and bad-mouthed me, complained about me to others, and was generally touchy to be around. One time I overheard her make the comment about my upcoming marriage, "I wish her luck. She's going to need it."

I was crushed. *Why would she say that?* I

wondered. *Why is she being so mean to me?*
It wasn't until a few months later, when I
heard she was getting a divorce, that the truth
of her situation dawned on me. I had taken
her harsh words and actions personally, but
truthfully they weren't meant that way. She
was speaking from her own pain.

When you encounter a toxic person, take
a moment to analyze what happened. Imagine
that they may have something going on
within them, that they may have a deep pain
or insecurity that they aren't handling well.
Perhaps something you said or did hit a nerve
or convicted them and so instead of dealing
with the root issue—them—they project it onto
you. Try to go deeper than just the surface of
your pain—that initial reaction you may feel.
You aren't excusing the behavior: you are
simply trying to understand it.

When I discovered what was happening in
Deborah's life, the pain she inflicted upon me
seemed to bother me less (notice, I didn't say
it completely disappeared!). Where hurt was,
pity and sympathy came; even forgiveness was
easier to give. She was living with deep pain,
and my upcoming nuptials were a constant
reminder that she had lost her joy. So for
reasons of jealousy, insecurity, or distance from
God, she chose to take out her hostility on me.
To make me the problem.

I've learned that we often find that it's easier to project pain onto someone else and make them the problem than to face our own issues. That's what Deborah did. Maybe that's what your toxic "buddies" are doing, too. So analyze what may be happening within them, and let that comprehension lead you a first step back into joy.

MAYBE THEY ARE AN ANSWER TO PRAYER.

Margaret[4] couldn't stand her mother-in-law. She was never good enough, smart enough, quick enough, fill-in-the-blank enough for her MIL's acceptance. Whenever Margaret spent any time with this woman, she usually ended up in tears or wanting to throw something sharp. In the midst of all that, Margaret, a devout Christian, constantly prayed for her faith to grow stronger and for her to become more like Christ. The more she prayed that prayer, however, the worse her relationship with Mommy-in-Law Dearest seemed to become. Until the worst possible circumstance occurred: her mother-in-law became too old and frail to continue to live on her own, and so she moved in with, you guessed it, Margaret.

I'm sure if she could have gotten hold of that Sleeping Beauty thorn from Maleficent, Margaret surely would have at least considered poking her MIL with it. Instead, she kept praying. She prayed for her mother-in-law, about her mother-in-law, against her mother-in-law. And still she prayed that God would shape her own character into that of Christ's.

One particularly bad day, Margaret had had enough. She was so frustrated that all she could do was go to the bathroom and take a shower. As the water and her tears poured over her, she felt a small voice whisper: *"You've asked to grow your faith, and I've given you an opportunity. Do you now not want to become more Christlike? Did you think becoming like Christ would be simple and sacrifice-free?"*

My first thought would have been, *Okay, maybe I don't really want to become more like Christ. Is there another option?*

But Margaret realized that perhaps her mother-in-law wasn't just in her life to be cared for, but because she was an answer to Margaret's character-building prayer.

There's a wonderful scene in *Evan Almighty* in which Evan's wife speaks with God (although she doesn't realize it's God) about her husband's questionable decision to build an ark. She's so upset about it that she considers leaving her marriage.

God's response:

"Let me ask you something. If someone prays for patience, you think God gives them patience? Or does he give them the opportunity to be patient? If he prayed for courage, does God give him courage, or does he give him opportunities to be courageous? If someone prayed for the family to be closer, do you think God zaps them with warm fuzzy feelings, or does he give them opportunities to love each other?"

You pray for patience and that day your children decide to dunk their feet in the toilet water and skate across your newly mopped floors. You pray to be kinder and the waitress is nasty and slow. You pray to be more Christlike and your mother-in-law moves in with you.

Interestingly enough, there's a flip side to this idea. Maybe *you're* an answer to *their* prayer! Maybe God is dealing with those people—Christians and non-Christians alike—and he's placed you in their lives to build their character, and they aren't handling it too well.

God answers our prayers by giving us opportunities to grow into those answers. Perhaps that's why you have those particular toxic peeps in your life.

During a conversation with my mom in which I moaned about a difficult relationship I was forced to endure, she gave me some wise advice: Ask yourself, *Why is that person in my life? Do they possibly serve a purpose? Why has God allowed them, yes, possibly even placed them on purpose, in my path? What can they teach me?*

I hated to admit it, but she was right. When I took the time to think through her advice, I found myself praying, *God, what can I learn through this experience? How can I best respond?* Then I went back to Hebrews 12:3: "Consider him who endured such opposition from sinful men, so that you will not grow weary and lose heart."

As I prayed and kept my eyes open to whatever God wanted to teach me, I was able to process those relationships differently. I knew not to take the situations personally, but they did still affect me, so I continued to pray and look to Jesus as my role model. The more I prayed, honestly, the Thorny Ones didn't get better. But *I* was different.

Find a Way to Get Away

Sometimes we just need to get away. Some people are *truly* toxic, and they can inflict abuse on us that not only damages us physically, mentally, and emotionally, but also damages our souls. Without a miraculous intervention from God, these people will never change. I think about the women I've encountered who have experienced domestic violence. Those things are never okay. God doesn't place an abuser in our lives to build our character. God is 100 percent against relationships with people who damage the core of who God made us to be.

The apostle Paul was clear: "Warn a divisive person once, and then warn them a second time. After that, *have nothing to do with them*. You may be sure that such people are warped and sinful; they are self-condemned" (Titus 3:10–11 NIV, emphasis added). Sometimes others will manipulate our faith to make us feel guilty about "having nothing to do with sinful people." You can love, have compassion for, and pray for someone very skillfully from afar. Only you know the toxic levels of infliction, so if you need to leave, then seek wise counsel and bravely do what you need to.

One Final Appeal That Will Make You Smile

If you're still struggling with how to handle toxic people, take some advice from one of my favorite Bible passages. This scripture from

Proverbs 25:18–22 (NIV) starts by showing us what toxic people do, offers a suggestion on how to respond, and then shows a certain stick-it-to-the-man-ness reward that will bring you comfort and a genuine smile.

> *Like a club or a sword or a sharp arrow*
>   *is one who gives false testimony*
>   *against a neighbor.*
> *Like a broken tooth or a lame foot*
>   *is reliance on the unfaithful in a time*
>   *of trouble.*
> *Like one who takes away a garment on a*
>   *cold day, or like vinegar poured on*
>   *a wound, is one who sings songs to*
>   *a heavy heart.*
> *If your enemy is hungry, give him food*
>   *to eat; if he is thirsty, give him water*
>   *to drink.*
> *In doing this, you will heap burning*
>   *coals on his head, and the* LORD *will*
>   *reward you.*

In other words, when toxic people interrupt your journey toward the happy life, the best response is to be kind. Sort of like killing them with kindness. It will drive them crazy— like heaping burning coals on their head. *Buahahahaha.*

The more you do that, the crazier they become! *But also:* when your motive is purely obedient, the more like Christ you become. Driving them crazy *and* becoming Christlike in the process? Yeah, it just doesn't get any better than that.

Who Is on Your Team?

So we know that it's okay to get away from toxic people, which will up our happiness levels exponentially. But what about the people we *choose* to hang around with? They can make or break us much more than the toxic people.

I often think about being on a relay team. I'm set and ready to run like the wind. My heel is jutted up against the starting block and I wait for my team members to run to me and then pass me the baton. I see the other team runners speeding down the track, passing their batons. My arm is stretched out, my palm open and ready to grasp and go. But if my team doesn't do their best, then there's no way I can succeed.

Paul says it like this: "Do not be misled: 'Bad company corrupts good character'" (1 Corinthians 15:33 NIV). Take an honest look at your friends. Do they support you, encourage you, challenge you, hold you accountable, seek your best?

Early in my professional acting career, I moved to Chicago with a sweet and wonderful friend, Amy. Amy is truly one of the best friends I've ever had. A strong Christian who isn't afraid to tell it like it is, she was in my life during some of our most definitive and growing years: those early twentysomethings. We shared a love of acting, old or foreign films, Ann Sather cinnamon rolls,[5] and Christ.

One evening as we were riding the bus home from a job we shared, I told her about this guy I'd liked for a long time who was kind of into me, but (looking back) wasn't really. Nevertheless, I was seriously considering going back to school to become a nurse, because he (a doctor) said he'd only marry a nurse.

Amy cut me off. "What are you doing?"

"What?"

"A nurse? Seriously? You don't even like the sight of blood."

"I can get used to it."

"So you're willing to give up on who you actually are in order to *maybe* get a guy who isn't even right for you? Tell me you aren't that stupid."

I could feel the blood rush to my face. Her words were making me angry.

You're supposed to be my friend and support my decisions, I thought. And then in a Holy Spirit flash of realization, *She* is *being my friend. And she's right. Wow, I'm such a dork.*

That night, I collected the nursing brochures and, along with that guy's phone number, dumped them all in the trash. Her words were difficult to hear, but she was absolutely right.

Compare that story to Dana's[6] situation: She started dating a guy who wasn't right for her. He wasn't a Christian, he was rude to her friends, and she changed whenever he was around. After several months, her group of friends decided to confront her with their concerns. She listened and then let them know that, while she appreciated their thoughts, she had everything under control—"You don't really know him like I do."

Eventually, against her friends' advice, she married him. Her marriage lasted less than ten years. After the divorce, she reconnected with her friends and admitted, "I should have listened. It would have saved me so much heartache."

Why do we have such trouble listening to our friends? We trust them to tell us if we look fat in an outfit; we listen to their recommendations on the best books and movies and restaurants. But then when it comes to the stuff that really matters—like relationships—we act as though they have IQs of 25.

Surround yourself with the right team players. Not just those who will say whatever you want to hear. Elvis did that—and he left the building. Permanently. Find those people you trust—and then trust *them*.

EMBRACING THE HAPPY LIFE:

❧ Who are the toxic people you have to deal with? How have you responded to them in the past? How could you respond differently after reading this chapter?

❧ Have your friends ever tried to warn you about a questionable relationship or action and you disregarded them? How did that turn out? Were they correct?

❧ In what ways can you be more proactive about listening to your friends' perspectives?

WHAT THE BIBLE HAS TO SAY:

"We can say with confidence, 'The Lord is my helper, so I will have no fear. What can mere people do to me?'" (Hebrews 13:6 NLT).

When you encounter a toxic person, take a moment to analyze what happened. Imagine that they may have something going on within them, that they may have a deep pain or insecurity that they aren't handling well.

[1] A disclaimer about this section—mostly because my mother thought I was being unusually cruel toward them. I happen to love the seven dwarfs, as you'll note from my kind words about them in the previous chapter. I find them charming, hilarious, and cute as a baby coon. I'm not dogging on these little hardworking diamond miners. Well, maybe a little, but just for the purpose of making my point.

[2] This is known as sarcasm. I know and adore many morning people. I have also threatened to put Fritos in their nostrils while they sleep and have my dog nuzzle up to them in the middle of the night. In true optimistic fashion, these happy people think my threat is so cute; they laugh and tell all their friends what a joyous thing they just heard me tell them.

[3] Name has been changed.

[4] Name has been changed.

[5] A specialty in the Lakeview neighborhood of Chicago, Ann Sather's restaurant was a regular hangout for us—unfortunately, as good as their food was, it didn't help our ongoing and eternal diets.

[6] Name has been changed.

Chapter 4

WHAT GREAT FAIRY-TALE PRINCESSES HAVE IN COMMON

Now faith is confidence in what we hope for and assurance about what we do not see.

HEBREWS 11:1 NIV

When I was very young, my parents (probably my mom) subscribed me to a Disney record membership in which I would get books and the audio of various fairy tales (this was a hundred years ago before DVDs or even videotapes). I would sit for hours and listen to the story of *Cinderella* with her fairy godmother and those wonderfully creative and cute mice, Gus and Jaq. I wasn't really even that impressed by the prince. I was more intrigued by singing the silliest song ever: "Bibbidi-Bobbidi-Boo."[1]

Even at that young age, I realized that I never heard Cinderella complain. She washed and mopped and dusted and scrubbed and ironed and worked her fingers to the bone, and nary a bad word fell from her lips. I, on the other hand, complained just because my mean mother wanted me to make my bed and keep my room tidy.

Years later, when *Beauty and the Beast* hit the big screen, I connected with Beauty for her love of books and good taste in men. She had the pick of the village, according to her suitor, Gaston, himself. But instead she chose the man who enjoyed her conversations. He may not have been a looker, but he respected her, even though he did have those bouts of beastliness and did technically keep her locked up. But he had great dinnerware that could sing and dance the best hospitality song around, "Be Our Guest."

Rapunzel was locked in a tower and seemed never to complain or argue when her mother refused to allow anything other than her long locks outside the tower walls.

As I've read fairy tales, I've noticed that, like most good stories, they have a few elements in common: girl in distress, she has some adventures (and unfair troubles), and she eventually wins the prince while the bad guys get their just deserts. But besides the basic storylines, I've noticed that they have some other commonalities.

Great dresses? Beautiful hair? Perfect bodies? Blemish-free skin? Okay, they do all have those things. Drat it all. But they have something else much more important in common: they have faith, they're resilient, and they're risk takers.

These women bounce back—under the worst, most dysfunctional circumstances. They don't get bitter. They stay hopeful, and in many cases they take the reins of their lives to grasp their happily ever after. Which fairy-tale princess ever sat around doing nothing and complaining and still ended up with Prince Charming? Not a one, my friend. Sure they need rescuing (we all need a savior), but none of them are passive in that rescue. They each play an important and powerful role. That's why we love them!

You may think, *Yeah, but those are fairy-tale people. They can have all kinds of bad things happen to them; they* aren't real.

Yep, you're right. But I do know of some people who had all kinds of bad things happen to them—and they *were* real, and *they* experienced wonderful happily ever afters.

The Foreigner Widow

Ruth was in a serious bind. She lived in a drought-stricken land, so she had no food. She'd lost her husband, she had no children, and to make matters worse, she was left only with her mother-in-law, also a widow— who happened to be whiny, complaining, and joyless; a woman who could up the my-suffering-is-worse-than-yours ante—and did.

After losing everything, including most of her hope, Ruth's MIL decided to pack up what was left of her life and travel back to her native homeland. She might be unhappy, but at least she could be unhappy among familiar surroundings and people and, if the rumors were correct, possibly food.

That meant Ruth had a choice: she could return to her own family, who was also suffering in the food shortage, or she could travel with her mother-in-law and become an immigrant. She'd be forced into a different culture and would face different people, different food, different holidays, different religion, different everything.

Something within Ruth, though, urged her to take a chance—even as her own MIL encouraged her *not* to accompany her. But Ruth pressed on and insisted, saying, "'Don't make me leave you, for I want to go wherever you go and to live wherever you live; your people shall be my people, and your God shall be my God; I want to die where you die and be buried there. May the Lord do terrible things to me if I allow anything but death to separate us'" (Ruth 1:16–17 TLB).

This wasn't a casual lunch date Ruth was making or a move across town. This wasn't a "Hey, I'll go with you and get some food, until the drought is over back here." This was a serious commitment. She was all in. Every single egg in one basket.

That meant she and MIL would have to walk—as in *on foot*, not by plane, train, or automobile—over mountains and into valleys, in a harsh and dangerous environment for two lone women. Not to mention, they couldn't stop at a McDonald's for a potty break and an iced tea, hit the Cracker Barrel for their vegetable plate extravaganza, or stop at the Desert Oasis outlet mall. And all this to go to an area Ruth had never been, to start a whole new life. With. Her. Mother-in-law.

On. Purpose.

When they arrived at their destination, the whole town became abuzz with the news. As the women, her friends, ran out to greet her, Ruth's MIL, Naomi, was in fine dramatic form. She told them, "'Don't call me Naomi; call me Bitter. The Strong One has dealt me a bitter blow. I left here full of life, and GOD has brought me back with nothing but the clothes on my back. Why would you call me Naomi [which means pleasant]? God certainly doesn't. The Strong One ruined me'" (Ruth 1:20–21 MSG). In essence, she was saying, *Forget that my name used to mean "pleasant." God has destroyed my life. I have nothing to be pleasant about*.

Those are some raw, honest, gut-wrenching, and emotionally melodramatic words. She *has* truly suffered, but she's not the only one. Let's not forget Ruth's suffering, which was just as deep and tragic. And while MIL was back in her homeland and community, Ruth had become a poor refugee, living with an emotionally inconsolable *mother-in-law*.

They moved into the old homestead, which

after so many years of neglect was a domestic nightmare. And leaving MIL with a broom, a mop, Mr. Clean, and any other cleaning supplies she could find, Ruth decided to leave MIL to the housework while she went out to find a job so they could eat.

Ruth landed in a field where she followed behind the workers and picked up any leftover grain that they'd missed. She was literally working for her survival. A long, hot day sifting prickly, itchy grain, bending and stretching enough to make Jillian Michaels exhausted. She worked hard, stayed focused, and refrained from complaining about the heat or the work.

And it "just so happened" that the rich field owner caught sight of her and heard about her work ethic. He was so impressed with her actions that he invited her to eat with him and his workers. He told his men to keep her safe and to add extra grain to her day's "wages."

Day after day she continued to work hard, proving her commitment to her MIL and gaining more respect and admiration from the Big Boss.

Eventually, at her MIL's urging, Ruth went, late at night, to where the boss was working, and when he fell asleep, she lay next to him. After something startled him awake and he caught sight of her next to him, he told her,

"'I will do for you all that you request, for all the people of my town know that you are a virtuous woman'" (Ruth 3:11 NKJV).

Soon they married, and she gave birth to a son who would become the grandfather to a famous king.

Ruth's Secret to Success

I love the above story.[2] When I start to read the first page, I feel as though it needs a "Once upon a time," because it fills me with all the awe and excitement of a Disney fairy tale. Only this "fairy tale" is real. I love the romance, the drama, the adventure. But mostly, I love that our protagonist princess, Ruth, models how to deal with life when troubles rock our world.

I can't imagine what she experienced—the grief, the angst, the hunger, the workload. Yet she managed it all with grace and grit. Even though the story doesn't spell out how joyful she was throughout her experience, I can *feel* her joy on every page. And as blessings began to show themselves to her and her MIL, I can *hear* her joy in every word.

And even better, Moaning Mother-in-law eventually caught the joy. At the end of the story, her friends entered the scene and rejoiced over the good things that had happened to her.

> The women of the town said to Naomi, "Praise the Lord, who has now provided a redeemer for your family! . . . May [this child] restore your youth and care for you in your old age. For he is the son of your daughter-in-law who loves you and has been better to you than seven sons!"
> RUTH 4:14–15 NLT

How can MIL not find happiness in that? I see her smile sweetly—becoming the "pleasant" Naomi again. Then she "took the baby and cuddled him to her breast. And she cared for him as if he were her own" (Ruth 4:16 NLT).

That happiness would never have come for Ruth—or her mother-in-law—had Ruth not exhibited a few character traits that we can grow in our own lives.

1. RUTH HAD FAITH.

You have to have faith to make the kind of trek that Ruth made. Sight unseen, moving to a different culture where they constantly reminded her that she was different, she went, *hoping* that life would offer something better. And it really didn't for a while. She had to work hard and endure living with a depressed mother-in-law. But she never allowed her faith to waver. And she didn't even know what to expect for a happily ever after. She simply stepped out, trusted God, and took each day as a new offering.

I can't say that I would have been able to hold on to hope and faith as well as Ruth did if I were in the same situation. But I can say that when we exercise our faith "muscles," they become stronger and we become better able to see beyond the present challenges, which in turn allows us to experience more faith and hope, which leads us to happiness.

Several years ago, I was in a miserable job. I felt as if I were living in the drought that Ruth and Naomi experienced. No rain. No growth. Only betrayals and politics and backstabbing. As year after year passed and the situation grew worse, I found myself struggling with my faith. I would often wonder, *How can this be where God wants me? Does he want me to stay here, or am I supposed to move on? How can I be happy while I'm so miserable?*

I remained, against my better judgment—mostly out of fear of not being able to find another job—and because of that decision, I added to my own demise. I gained sixty pounds. I began to experience migraines and other health issues. I was tired all the time. And my displeasure became evident in my attitude. (*Bitter* would have been a good name for me.) I still believed strongly in my work, and I did it to the best of my ability; it was all the other workplace drama and decisions that beat me up.

Finally, after I'd evaded a scandalous number of layoffs, my number came up and I was let go. When on a Monday morning my supervisor informed me of the company's decision and that my last day would be that Friday, I could have reached over the table and kissed her. I couldn't have been more relieved. *Freedom!*

I joked with my husband that I wanted to leave her office and skip back to mine. Immediately I felt lighter, happier, calmer, and less tempted to eat a box of Krispy Kremes. But by midday, panic began to settle in.

What in the world am I going to do? What if I never find another job? What if I fail? The what-ifs came fast and furious.

Tuesday morning, while I was getting ready for work, I heard an unmistakable voice speak to me. Though it wasn't audible, it was as loud as it could have been without being audible. It said simply, *"I will not let you fall."*

At that moment, I had a choice. I could trust, by faith, to believe those words—an all-or-nothing, all-eggs-in-one-basket kind of belief. Or I could nod and "believe" and then continue down a path of fear and anxiety. In an instant, I said aloud, "Okay, Lord, if you've said that, then I will choose to believe."

Every single moment after that, my faith grew as I watched God remain faithful to those words. I started my own business, and in the days since, I've never gone a day without work. As I finish one project and I have a moment when I wonder if that's the last one I'll ever see, in the eleventh hour, the next project shows up. And now when I finish a project and the next one isn't on the horizon, I've found that my faith says, *Okay, God, I know the next one is coming. Send it when you choose.* And he does. Every time. He doesn't provide because I'm such a "talented" worker; he provides because he is faithful. So my faith grows because I know he can be trusted.

When I chose faith that Tuesday in my bathroom, that choice paved a way for me to grow my faith with each new experience. And as I've seen God's faithfulness, more and more the fear has dissipated and a deep, abiding joy has made its home in my life.

My friend Liz Curtis Higgs says it this way, "When you and I see nothing but dirt and sweat and work, God sees joy and fulfillment right around the corner. While we fret and worry, God says, 'Trust me.' "[3] Faith is choosing, when we can't see the outcome, to believe that

God will not let us fall. And when we cling to that faith and hope, as Ruth did, joy *cannot help* but follow.

2. RUTH WAS RESILIENT.

Ruth could have easily thrown in the proverbial towel when her hubby died. Husbandless and childless, she could have fallen into the throes of despair and chosen a life of misery. In some sense, Naomi did that. After her husband and sons died, Ms. Bitter MIL determined to suffer. She had a bit of self-preservation when she discovered that food was plentiful back in her home country. But she refused any help to get there, trying to turn her daughters-in-law away from taking the journey with her. Perhaps by going it alone, she would have died en route; perhaps that was her game plan.

"Just let me die!" The pain is so great, the only option we may desire is death. That plea was very real for a mom I know who recently lost her fifteen-year-old daughter to a rare disease. Within a few months, she also lost her mother and then, less than six months after that, she lost her job. To add insult to injury, her father died three months later. Any one of those tragedies is a crushing weight in and of itself. But four in a row can push someone over the edge. My friend could have died—physically, emotionally, spiritually—but fortunately, her strong faith also provided the ability for her to become resilient.

She started a blog to share her story and to keep her daughter's memory alive. She continued to work in her church prayer ministry. She dove into life as a mother to her son. She met friends for coffee. She told her honest, raw feelings, but always then bookended them with praise toward a God who loves her and who loves those she lost. She inspires me because she chose the difficult path of getting up every day and looking for glimpses of God's goodness to her.

"I don't understand," she told me one day over lunch. "And maybe that's the point to this whole thing. Maybe I'm not supposed to. If I understood, why would I need faith? If I understood, would I be able to handle the reality of it all? Probably not, and I can find peace and a bit of happiness in knowing that, ultimately, I'm where God wants me to be."

I know another woman who has been the most resilient person I've ever met. Phyllis was diagnosed with breast cancer in 1993. "I thought I'd die. Everyone around me thought so, too—especially people who knew people who'd died of it."[4] She thought the doctors caught it all, until two years later when a bone scan showed a suspicious spot on her hip bone. Then it returned in 2001. "While round two of breast cancer initially knocked me for a loop, I wasn't down long."[5]

But in the midst of fighting for her life, she found herself also fighting for her marriage when she discovered that her husband was having an affair. So she doubled down and fought hard. Her cancer went into remission, she got divorced, and soon her cancer returned. She fought again. It again went into remission. And it returned. She fought again. Over and over she battled that foe.

"You've got a wonderful stubborn streak in you," I told her. "I think that's what's kept you alive."

She smiled and shrugged. "Sometimes I think it would be better if I just gave up. It would be easier."

"But you're a fighter. And you have more to do in this life."

"I guess I do, God willing. Until he takes me home, I will continue to fight as hard as I can."

I saw her as naturally brave, until I read a beautiful article she wrote about her experience in which she admitted that she'd worked hard to become courageous—but that hadn't meant that she didn't experience her share of tears.

When people ask why God would give me breast cancer twice, I often say,

*"Why would he give me health? One
is no more deserved than another." . . .
[Yet] there definitely is a time for tears.
You cry on the elevator ride from the
doctor's office after he's put you at the
top of his "hit list" for surgery. You cry
when your husband wraps his arms
around you, trying to ease the blow of
a biopsy report. You cry on the phone
when you're telling your kids. You cry
when Mom tells you, "I wish I could
have this instead of you."*

*But there's a time to stop mourning,
too, and get back to life.*

*One way to do that is to get back to
whatever it is God's called you to do.*[6]

That acknowledgment made her *even stronger*
in my eyes. That's what resilience is: it's getting
back up and never giving up, even when you
know you could potentially get thrown down
again.

Why work so hard at resilience? Because,
as Phyllis writes:

*The best way to beat back the enemy
is to put every fear into the hands of
the God who made us, sustains us,
and controls whatever happens to
us. He knew I'd have cancer. In his*

*unfathomable wisdom, he allowed it
to happen for reasons that are only
beginning to become apparent to me.
And in his boundless grace, God is
using cancer to bless me and those
around me. Even if it so ravages my
body that I no longer have the strength
to go on living, I'll still win the battle.*[7]

Recently I reconnected with Phyllis, and she's still plugging away. Every day she wakes up ready to take on life in its wrestling match. But she is filled with joy—the joy of recognizing the gifts that God overflows into her life. And that has brought her a happily ever after every day.

The same goes for our "Princess" Ruth. She didn't know where her journey would lead her, but she said yes to the promise of everyday hope. She was resilient. And she was rewarded for it.

3. RUTH WAS WILLING TO RISK.

Ruth risked going to a foreign land to live. She risked finding work in a stranger's field. She risked obeying her mother-in-law's request to lie down at the feet of a man and ask him to marry her and care for her. Scandalous!

I would have balked if my mother-in-law—or anyone!—told me to go out on a huge limb and make such a request. I'd feel as if I were reliving my ninth-grade year in which I told Andy Williams's brother, who was a senior, that I had a crush on him. To which he replied awkwardly, "Uh, thanks," and then avoided me like the plague for the rest of his high school career. Thankfully for him and me that was only one year.

Never again. *No* thank you.

But Ruth trusted her mother-in-law and took the risk. And boy, oh boy, did that one pay off.

We'll talk more about becoming a risk taker in the next chapter. But for now, as we look at Ruth's life, we see the importance and power of taking a chance: she had to take action in order for God to accomplish his will not only in her life but in the life of an entire nation.

Imagine, had she not stepped out in faith and trusted God and the unlikely Naomi, she might not have married Boaz or had a baby (Obed), who would never have married and had a baby (Jesse), who would have never had a son, David—the David who was a man after God's own heart (Acts 13:22)—who became the famous King David of Jewish history and acclaim. So much history set in place—all because she was willing to take a risk.

The Hall of Famers

Ruth isn't the only one in the Bible who strove

to gain the happily-ever-after life. Hebrews 11 gives a beautiful rundown of people who took chances, trusted God, were resilient, and held on to hope at all costs. The author starts this hall of fame by pointing out that each person made this model list because of his or her faith.

"Now faith is confidence in what we hope for and assurance about what we do not see," the author tells us. "This is what the ancients were commended for" (Hebrews 11:1–2 NIV). And to prove their merit as the faith masters, the author begins his list:

- ❧ Abel, for his sacrificial offering to God.

- ❧ Enoch, who pleased God, "and it is impossible to please God without faith. Anyone who wants to come to him must believe that God exists and that he rewards those who sincerely seek him" (Hebrews 11:6 NLT).

- ❧ Noah, for obeying God when he felt led to build an unbelievably large boat when it had never rained.

- ❧ Abraham, who obeyed God's leading and left his home to go to another land. "He went without knowing where he was going" (Hebrews 11:8 NLT).

- ❧ Sarah, because she "believed that God would keep his promise" (Hebrews 11:11 NLT).

✤ Isaac, who "promised blessings for the future to his sons" (Hebrews 11:20 NLT).

He continues his list: Jacob, Joseph, Moses' parents, Moses, the Hebrews who "went right through the Red Sea as though they were on dry ground" (Hebrews 11:29 NLT), Rahab the prostitute, and the impressive list goes on.

"By faith," he continues, "these people overthrew kingdoms, ruled with justice, and received what God had promised them" (Hebrews 11:33 NLT).

They held on to faith and were resilient. And they surround us as a "great cloud of witnesses" (Hebrews 12:1 NIV)—they testify to us that we can live happily ever after. They cheer us on: "We did it, you can, too!"

Choose to get back up over and over again. Choose to live by faith, to hope, to trust.

EMBRACING THE HAPPY LIFE:

- ❀ Would you consider yourself resilient? Why or why not?

- ❀ Which of the Hall of Famers did you most connect with? What can you learn from how they handled life's circumstances?

- ❀ In what ways could you build your faith?

WHAT'S IN IT FOR ME?

- ❀ Keep focused on your inner worth rather than the external circumstances. Even though Ruth was a foreigner and they labeled her as such, that was not her identity.

Choose to get back up
over and over again.
Choose to live by faith,
to hope, to trust.

[1] While I'm not even sure what it means, I'm humming it now as I type. "Alakazoola midgetkaboola bibbidi-bobbidi-boo." Unfortunately, those aren't the words. Much to my chagrin I've discovered that I've spent the past several decades singing false lyrics. For the record, I just learned the actual words are "Salagadoola mechicka boola, bibbidi-bobbidi-boo. Put 'em together and what have you got? Bibbidi-bobbidi-boo." Put 'em together and what have you got? A whole bunch of nonsense writing that paid some handsome royalties, that's what. But I digress.

[2] For more details about Ruth and her MIL, read the biblical account of Ruth, in the Old Testament book of the same name.

[3] Liz Curtis Higgs, *The Girl's Still Got It* (Colorado Springs, CO: WaterBrook Press, 2012), 80.

[4] Phyllis Ten Elshof, "Taking on Breast Cancer," *Today's Christian Woman,* March/April 2002, http://www.todayschristianwoman.com/articles/2002/march/8.74.html.

[5] Ibid.

[6] Ibid.

[7] Ibid.

Chapter 5

CINDERELLA: CARPE DIEM!
(CARPE PUMPKIN!
CARPE THAT SHOE!)

*We are not of those who shrink
back and are destroyed, but of
those who believe and are saved.*

HEBREWS 10:39 NIV 1984

ittle Cinder Maid had a rough life. Mom died. Dad died.[1] An orphan, she was left to the mercy of malicious step-relations who treated her like a servant. But Cinderella didn't let her past misfortune or present circumstances get in the way of her pursuing, yes, seizing upon the could-bes.

When Fairy Godmother appeared, Cinderella didn't think twice about accepting her invitation for an extreme makeover. And by obediently following Fairy Godmother's bibbidi-bobbidi-boo orders to leave the castle ball by midnight, she guaranteed herself a position as the future Mrs. Prince Charming.

Cinderella said yes: to the dress, to the risk, and to the reward.

As our model, she now tells us, "Take hold of the moment! Don't allow fear of the unknown to get in the way of becoming who you were rightfully created to be."

Amen, I say. Risk reaching for the stars. Risk for the possibility of a stronger and brighter future. Risk for the wisdom that comes through the success and the failure. Risk for the promise that stagnation won't take over in your spirit and soul. Take a chance!

But I also know it isn't always as easy as Cinderella makes it seem. For instance, whenever I've taken a risk, I've never once met a mouse who could sew. I've never seen a pumpkin with a built-in transmission. And I've never met a singing and jolly fairy godmother who showed up waving a wand and offering me glass stilettos. It's usually a little more complicated. And less animated.

My friend Kim took a chance when she and her husband, Jahn, decided to adopt a little boy from Ukraine. Everything seemed to go according to plan. They submitted their paperwork, paid their fees, went through the background checks and home inspection, and then flew to Ukraine to greet their family's new addition. But once in Ukraine, things started to fall apart. The adoption went through, but a corrupt prosecutor, who didn't want an American to take one of Ukraine's children, challenged the adoption orders. That meant that Kim's son, Jake, wasn't allowed to leave the country.

Rather than return home without her son, she chose to remain in Ukraine for a year—where things only continued to spiral downward. She ended up hiding from the authorities, had a warrant out for her arrest (because she refused to return Jake to the orphanage), and suffered bouts of loneliness and spiritual despair.

People kept encouraging her to leave and go home, that things would work themselves out, that she and Jahn could always adopt another child, that this was too difficult. She should just let it go.

But she was all in. She had taken a chance and she wasn't going to back out. She knew that God was with her in this journey—even though she didn't always sense his presence or see his hand at work.

After a year, an arrest, and a dramatic escape, she made it home with her son. Today, she'll tell you it was the hardest—but the best—thing she's ever done.

"Taking that risk and committing to it—when everyone else thought I was crazy—was something I'm glad I did," Kim told me. "I learned so much about faith and about what real, gut-level joy looks like. And best of all, I have a beautiful son. By obeying God to take that chance in Ukraine, I learned the extent God will go to move mountains for one abandoned child, and how God will stop at nothing to show how much he loves and cares for orphans."[2]

If we want to experience mind-blowing joy, then we have to be willing to take risks.

Most of Us Prefer Reaching for the Sure Thing

When I worked as an editor for a national

magazine, I would often attend writers' conferences and meet with aspiring authors. I loved connecting with these thoughtful and talented people who had stories to share. Part of my responsibility at each conference was to take fifteen-minute individual appointments so that writers could "pitch" their ideas to me to see if I liked their work and would be willing to let them submit their writing to my publication.

Often during these appointments, newbie writers would show up and literally shake as they handed me their articles to evaluate. Their voices would quiver; they would stutter. I even had a few tear up.

In those cases, I would reach my hand over and gently touch them.

"It's okay. I don't usually bite," I'd tell them. If they only knew how unimpressive I really was, they wouldn't be so terrified. But I also understood they were taking a huge risk by showing me their "babies"—and I had the power to put their name in print or to crush their dreams. On my side, it was a humbling, sobering knowledge to have that kind of power. On their side, however, it was a humbling and potentially sobering gamble.

I found great writers and thrived on mentoring them and publishing their work. Inevitably, however, as much as I tried to avoid it, I know I did crush some sensitive hearts.

Incidentally, when I first started my work as an editor, I kept a file of every person to whom I'd responded that I wanted to see their work. When the writer submitted an article, I would pull their information from my file and attach it to their new stuff. But as the years went by, my file grew wider and wider, because so many authors never sent me their articles.

At one conference I mentioned my frustration over that growing file, and one brave author explained it to me.

"It's a big obstacle just to submit our idea to you," he confessed sheepishly. "If you say yes, then we have something to hold on to that isn't a rejection. We can tell our friends and family that an editor liked our writing so much that she requested to see our work. And everyone is impressed."

"But that's only half the reward."

He shrugged. "Half the reward is better than being rejected completely."

These folks—many of them truly gifted—never saw their bylines in print because they allowed fear of failure to overcome the reward of taking a committed risk.

These writers are simply a microcosm of how many of us operate our everyday lives. We have dreams, passions, talents, but we keep them hidden away in the dark vaults of our spirit for fear of failure or heartache. It's easier to yearn for success without pursuing it. We play it safe—the death knell of every dream.

In the dinosaur days before I became a writer and editor, I worked as a professional actress. All through high school and college, I auditioned and nailed each part. I received accolades and great reviews for my performances. My goal: to be on Broadway. When I graduated, I hit the world by storm and performed in touring shows and outdoor theaters and documentaries.

But the truth was that after a few years into being out of college and on my own, when a friend and I moved to Chicago to hit it big, I blew it. I settled into an office job and rarely auditioned. I did a few professional theater shows and a few performances at community theaters (big fish in a small pond stuff), but I never really took the risk to pursue the dream of landing on Broadway. I used all the excuses: I need to pay my rent, I have a cold, I don't really like that director. But really, I didn't take the risk because I got comfortable in the status quo. It was too much work and too difficult.

And if I were really honest, if I risked it all— really worked out and put myself out there, gave it everything I had—and I didn't succeed. . .

I was afraid to fail. Doing college and community theater is one thing, but Broadway? What if I wasn't really as good as everybody said? What if I really couldn't act?

I was willing to neglect and throw away the dream and talent that I'd had for so many years—all because I wanted to play it safe. I took a few risks—I joined my church's drama ministry, for instance. But they were still "safe" risks.

Playing it safe means that we remain stuck in a go-nowhere job, that we stagnate in our relationships, that we never travel to the places we've always wanted to visit, that we don't use and stretch the talents our Creator endowed us with, that we "half risk."

Taking chances never guarantees success. At least in the way we may view it. That's why so many of us prefer the "risk" of playing it safe. It may have been better to have loved and lost for Alfred, Lord Tennyson, who wrote that statement, but it's easier, safer, and less painful never to have loved at all.

Taking the Right Risks

I'm not a risk taker. Left-hand, green arrow-less turns at busy intersections make me jittery. I'll go to the Grand Canyon and enjoy the view, but don't even think about trying to pull me out onto the glass-bottomed platform to look a mile straight down. I don't care that it's safe. I don't care that thousands of people do it every year and live to tell the tale. I. Do. Not. Care.

Mixing peanut butter with jelly is about as risky as I like to get.

On the other hand, my husband's natural bent leans toward taking risks. He is a former deputy sheriff. He brought motorcycles into the fleet of police vehicles. He chased down bad guys doing well over 100 mph on said motorcycles.

Just hearing him tell the stories makes me break a sweat and reach for a Pepcid. But he loves that stuff. He loves pushing the boundaries.

Once when we visited Yellowstone, he decided to test a geyser basin. The sign clearly stated something about not touching the boiling hot water.

"I bet it really isn't that hot," he said, as he stepped off the path and knelt down beside the aquamarine-colored *bubbling* liquid.

"But the sign. . ." I stated lamely, knowing he wasn't going to heed my warning and silently praying that our vacation wouldn't include a trip to the local emergency room.

He dipped his finger into the pool and brought it up. "Yep. That's seriously hot." His finger displayed a lovely bright pink tinge the rest of the day.

While some risks are just stupid (see above story), some risks are worth taking—if we want to live a happy life.

My friends Ben and Kayla[3] have a great marriage. But for years Ben was an alcoholic. He could usually hide it well, but eventually it overtook his life to the point that he got fired from his job. For years Kayla had harped on him to stop drinking, but she never really took the risk of laying down a clear boundary. When they had to file for bankruptcy, Kayla finally pulled an intervention and told Ben that either he had to stop drinking or she would leave him. He sought help, quit drinking, and became a totally different person. He started his own business that became successful within a few years. He started exercising and lost weight. He began to appreciate his wife and their marriage.

They both took good risks. Kayla's risk could have ended by her losing her marriage and everything she loved. But she chose to proceed, knowing the consequences of failure but also knowing the reward could be great.

Ben took a risk by seeking help for his addiction. He could have refused and lost everything. But the reward, which he couldn't see clearly in the midst of his troubles, brought incredible joy to him and to everyone around him.

How do we know which risks are the right

ones to take to help us avoid undue painful consequences?

1. DO YOUR DUE DILIGENCE.

Reaching for our happily ever after isn't simply about taking risks; it's about taking wise risks, strategizing, discerning, and praying through the possibilities at hand.

For instance, I met a woman at a conference once who wanted to be a writer, so this single mom quit her job and started to write. Now a year later, when I met her, she had no funds to pay her bills, had no published work, and no hope. When she met with me, she was desperate. Unfortunately, as I read through her writing samples, I saw that her work was unrefined and amateurish. It didn't hold together well and she was unable to articulate her points—all issues that she could have tackled by learning and honing her craft. But instead of taking the time to do that, she'd jumped right into the shark tank—and the sharks were chomping at her kneecaps.

"Have you taken any writing classes or joined a writers' group?" I asked her.

No.

"Had you published anything before you quit your job or worked to build your network?"

No.

She'd simply had a passion, felt God

leading her in that direction, and chucked her job (and her brain, apparently). Her risk proved devastating. All because she chose to take an unwise risk.

A better risk for her? Do all the things I'd asked her about—while still working. Build a network of writing connections, get bylines in print, procure regular paying assignments, *then* quit your job. The risk is still the same (quitting her job to pursue something she loves), but she's *more prepared* for the potential consequences as well as the rewards.

Cops risk their lives every day when they go on duty—but they're prepared for the risks: they've been trained in firing weapons, pursuing suspects, eyeballing crime scenes. They don't simply watch an episode of *Flashpoint*, put on a uniform, and then head out to battle the world's worst. If they did that and neglected to do their due diligence, they would have taken unwise risks—which could potentially be fatal. The writer wannabe was sort of in the same camp: she hadn't done her due diligence.

2. ASK GOD FOR WISDOM TO DETERMINE THE BEST RISK.

Several years ago, while on vacation, my husband and I visited Deadwood, South Dakota, in the heart of the Black Hills. We discovered that almost every establishment included gambling "opportunities." One restaurant had a small casino attached to it, so after we noshed, we decided to try our hand at playing the slots. We took a small amount of money and headed toward the cashier to get quarters to use in the machines. But as we waited in line, I overheard a conversation between two women that made my stomach churn.

> Woman #1: What am I going to do? That was the last of my money.
> Friend: You'll get it back.
> Woman #1: [*in tears*] I even spent the money I had to pay my bills! I. . .I—
> Friend: [*in a concerned voice*] They take credit cards. You just need one break and you'll get it all back. Did you bring your Visa?

Cliff ahead. Runaway horses. And that woman was saddled in.

First of all, the woman's friend was no friend (we talked in an earlier chapter about how the people we surround ourselves with impact our happiness level). She needed a friend who would hold her accountable and warn her of the nearing cliff. Second, this woman could have used a healthy dose of discernment.

She failed in both cases. I'm not sure what she did, because Scott and I left soon after that. But I have a heavy feeling that she pulled out her credit card and pushed it to its limit.

In 1 Kings, Solomon has been crowned king of Israel and he feels the weight of that responsibility. He prays an honest and beautiful prayer as he says, "Give your servant a discerning heart . . . to distinguish between right and wrong."

And God "was pleased that Solomon had asked for this. So God said to him, 'Since you have asked for this and not for long life or wealth for yourself. . .I will do what you have asked. I will give you a wise and discerning heart'" (1 Kings 3:9–12 NIV).

That's taking a wise risk. Rather than rushing in first and thinking later, we need to ask God to lead us into the right choices and then wait for him to give us that direction.

Lisa[4] was engaged to a man whom everybody loved. He got along well with her family. He was respected in his job. He volunteered at his church. He was Mr. Perfect. . .for someone other than Lisa.

While she respected him and enjoyed his company and friendship, she'd felt pressured to continue in the relationship because everyone kept telling her what a catch he was. She struggled with herself, wondering if she was just being too picky, since he really was the perfect guy. But she also had dreams to travel the world and work for an international justice organization, something she wouldn't be able to do if she married him.

Finally, she decided to pray about the situation. She asked God to fill her with wisdom to make the right decision. She knew if she broke up with her fiancé, she might never meet another Mr. Right. She wondered if she would spend her life alone. She wondered if she did marry him, would she lose the things she was passionate about.

As she asked for a clear sense of discernment, God put her in several situations that helped her make her decision. The first was that she had an honest conversation with her fiancé, in which she talked about her dreams and whether they would work within their marriage. The second was that she met an old friend who introduced her to someone who worked in the field she wanted to be in.

Lisa decided to take the risk and break her engagement. As difficult as that was, she felt at peace with it. Soon, she landed an interview with her friend's friend, got the job, and moved overseas. Though she's still unmarried, she's fulfilled and happy because she's using the desires and gifts God placed within her.

I'm not suggesting that if you're unhappy

in a relationship—particularly a marriage—that you should "take a risk" and get a divorce. More often than not, that road is an unwise risk—for numerous reasons.[5] What I'm suggesting with humility is to take a risk by recommitting, by doubling up and giving more to your marriage. The same goes with a friendship, a neighborhood, a church. I know too many people who church hop because their current church doesn't "fulfill their likes." Sometimes the real risk comes in staying and sticking it out. That church may be the unlikely instrument that brings you spiritual growth and maturity.

God will answer our prayer for discernment. The Bible assures us that "if any of you lacks wisdom, you should ask God, who gives generously to all without finding fault, and it will be given to you. But when you ask, you must believe and not doubt, because the one who doubts is like a wave of the sea, blown and tossed by the wind" (James 1:5–6 NIV). We simply need to ask and then to believe that God will give us the wisdom we need to take the right risks.

GOOD RISK/NOT-SO-GOOD RISK

Good risk: Making a solid case in front of your boss of why you need a promotion/raise.
Not-so-good risk: Asking for a promotion/raise after you post on Facebook that your boss passed gas in the weekly meeting.

Good risk: Asking your mother-in-law to lunch to get to know her better.
Not-so-good risk: Taking her to a seafood place when she's allergic to shellfish and then making her pay the bill.

Good risk: Saying yes to God's nudge to do short-term missions work.
Not-so-good risk: Doing the missions work by making reservations at a Bahamas Sandals resort with plans to do your devos by the pool.

Good risk: Deciding you want to spice up your marriage by getting closer to your hubby.
Not-so-good risk: Parading in front of the television set in the middle of March Madness.

The Secret Risk Ingredient

Risks require courage, sure, but more so, they involve humility. Happy life risk taking requires that we give up our need to be right, to be thought of in a certain more-glamorous way, to chuck our pride, and be willing to lose everything, as Jesus did, for the "joy set before him" (Hebrews 12:2).

After my layoff, when I saw how faithful God was in that circumstance, I realized that I should have quit that job years before. (Two summers earlier I'd been offered—unsolicited—three jobs and I turned them all down. Stupid crazy, huh?) But I was afraid of taking that risk; I was afraid that I wouldn't succeed, that I would jump from one bad job into another. Sort of the mentality that *It's better to stick with the devil you know than take a chance on the devil you don't know*. And why? Because of fear. But what's the root of that? Pride. I didn't quit and take the chance of succeeding or failing because I wasn't humble enough to deal with the potential to fail. I didn't trust that God wouldn't let me fall. That's pride at its saddest. Shame on me—I can say that now with 20/20 hindsight.

I've known women who wouldn't take a stand against their husbands, who were using pornography or sleeping around, because they were afraid of what they'd lose. So they remained stagnant, unhappy, unhealthy, and married to someone they couldn't trust. (I knew a woman who discovered her husband was using pornography, but she wouldn't tell the church leaders—to get him help and hold him accountable—because "it would make him look bad." *That's* pride, my friend.)

I've known women who wouldn't say no to their children's bad behavior because they didn't want their children to dislike them. They wouldn't take the risk that could potentially lead their kids to become stronger, healthier, and less entitled adults because they wouldn't allow themselves to see past the short term.

I've known women who wouldn't go out on dates with really cool guys because they didn't trust the guys to be "good enough."

I've known women who quit college for fear of not getting good enough grades.

I've known women who refused to get involved in a small group at church and risk community and intimacy with other people for fear that they'd be hurt.

Risk is difficult. No doubt about it. But too often pride keeps us from even trying. We don't want others to see us possibly fail. What do we fear? Failure? Vulnerability? Betrayal? All things that sit smack-dab in the midst of the pride pool. That pride keeps us from a happy life. It keeps us stuck and stagnant.

But the opposite of pride offers us amazing opportunities for happiness: humility. When I say, *I trust God. I don't know where he's leading, but I'm going to give this an honest-to-goodness try. I'm going to allow myself to be vulnerable and real and raw. I choose to trust. I choose to step out into the unknown—* that's when we open ourselves to humility. That's when happiness has a real and lasting chance.

One of the greatest opportunities to show humility and earn its reward is through love. Not simply romantically—although that's a hugey-huge risk. Giving ourselves in the most intimate way to another person, willingly offering them the ability to hurt us by laying open our vulnerabilities—that's a risk a lot of people have tried, and frankly, it didn't bring a happily ever after. The pain keeps them from getting back on that proverbial horse and riding (resilience and faith). But what do we miss when we say no to the risk of loving a friend, stranger, pain-in-the-neck neighbor, family member, church member? We cocoon ourselves from being hurt; we refuse the humility it takes to offer ourselves up for the adventure of loving and receiving love, of serving another human being and compassionately giving to someone in need. That cocoon of pride and comfort keep out raw, awkward, delightful, wondrous happiness—not just the feeling of *being* happy, but also the happiness of growing into a more mature, more compassionate, more loving, more giving, more honoring, more respectful person.

The All-Practical "Why Not?"

Author and speaker Barbara Rosberg told me one time that she changed her entire life when she began responding to different opportunities and requests with a simple phrase: *Why not?*

If her husband wanted her to go somewhere with him and she was loaded down with chores and a long to-do list, she took the risk and said, "Why not?" And she'd go.

She started to take the risk that those two words brought and found that her life became fuller, richer, more joy filled. She applied it to how she dealt with her work, her clients, her grandchildren, even strangers (within limits— see how to take wise risks above).

Her practical take encouraged me in my

own risk-taking ventures toward happiness. So several years ago, when my husband, Scott, wanted to buy a motorcycle from a guy in downstate Illinois and wanted me to accompany him to pick it up, I said, "Sure, why not?" We would make it a minivacation: just the two of us, riding a motorcycle through corn fields and along the mighty Mississippi.

Not even twenty-four hours into picking up the bike, we were involved in an accident. As we started to turn into a restaurant parking lot, a driver who was speeding and we think texting saw us too late, slammed on his brakes, skidded more than twenty-five feet, and smashed into our bike. The impact sent me soaring into the air in one direction and pinned Scott under the bike as he and the machine slid about twenty feet in the other direction.

We were fortunate that neither of us was terribly injured (although my elbow still aches whenever the weather changes). But now we had a dilemma. We were more than four hours from home and the only way to get there was to get back on that bike. Or we could walk. I didn't fancy either option. I knew I had to get back on. But that was a huge risk, because we weren't sure now how the bike would handle or how damaged it was (it ended up being totaled), but also because now I was afraid of the other drivers. If one driver hadn't paid attention and hit us, how many others were out there? And would we be so fortunate the next time?

Everything within my risk-averse spirit screamed, *Walk! Rent a car! Take the bus! Call Mom! Just don't get back on that motorcycle!* I could have allowed my emotions to take control—and I would have been justified. But I also knew we didn't have extra cash sitting around for a car rental. And I couldn't ask someone to drive all that way to come get me.

I sucked it up and gave myself a pep talk: *Ginger, Scott was a cop. He's a good and safe driver. You can't live with a worst-case scenario mentality that keeps you from living life to the fullest. Now, buck up and get out there.*

But what if it does *become a worst-case scenario?* my paranoid self nagged back.

What if it does? Ultimately, you'll be okay whatever happens, the rational, risk-taking side retorted.

We have an adversary who would like nothing more than to paralyze us into paranoia so that we never take a risk. But if we never risk, we never gain the reward.

The rational, risk-taking side won. I pumped myself up, said, "Oh why not?" and got back on the motorcycle and we drove home. I'm so grateful that I did that. I felt ecstatic when we pulled into our driveway. One, we survived.

But also because I took the risk and faced my fears. And it made it easier the next time Scott asked me to take a risk. I knew the worst-case stuff, but I also knew the rewards of spending time close to my husband.

So Get Out There and Carpe Diem!

One of the classic movies that inspires its viewers to take risks to live a happily-ever-after life is *Dead Poets Society*, starring the late Robin Williams. The movie takes place in a private, all-boys boarding school in the 1950s, during a time and place when these students' parents had already determined their future roles and vocations. Into their midst walks Professor John Keating, the new English teacher, who encourages the boys to go against everyone's expectations and pursue their own dreams. As each boy heeds Keating's advice, his worldview is broadened and his life forever changed.[6]

Some of the best quotes from the movie have gained lasting influence:

❀   You must strive to find your own voice.

Because the longer you wait to begin, the less likely you are to find it at all. Thoreau said, "Most men lead lives of quiet desperation." Don't be resigned to that. Break out![7]

❀ Carpe diem, seize the day. Gather ye rosebuds while ye may.[8]

❀ I went to the woods because I wanted to live deliberately. I wanted to live deep and suck out all the marrow of life. . . . To put to rout all that was not life; and not, when I had come to die, discover that I had not lived.[9]

Suck out all the marrow of life.
Carpe diem.
Seize the day.

Ruth seized the day, as we saw in the previous chapter. My friend Kim seized the day. Cinderella seized the day. And the writer of Hebrews encourages us to do the same. Writing to the first-century church, who were under intense persecution, he calls them (and us) to take the risk and stand firm in their faith, because "we are not of those who shrink back and are destroyed, but of those who believe and are saved" (Hebrews 10:39 NIV 1984).

How are we able to take risks? The biblical writers give us that answer, too: we are able to take risks because "the Lord is my helper; I will not be afraid. What can mere mortals do to me?" (Hebrews 13:6 NIV, quoting Psalm 118:6–7).

And perhaps that's the biggest and best reason of all for us to take risks for our happily ever afters: because when we walk in faith, staying close in our relationship to God, he will lead us and protect us.

EMBRACING THE HAPPY LIFE:

- ❧ Are you more of a natural risk taker or do you prefer to play it safe? In what ways has that personality type served you well? In what ways has it hindered your happiness?

- ❧ Think about a time when you took an unwise risk. How did that turn out? What did you learn from that experience?

- ❧ If you're more of a play-it-safe person, what keeps you from taking more risks?

- ❧ Do you believe pride keeps you from risking?

- ❧ If you were in Cinderella's shoes, so to speak, would you risk the wrath of the stepmother and pursue the potential of a brighter future? Or would you play it safe and offer excuses for why you can't go to the ball?

WHAT'S IN IT FOR ME?

- ✿ This week, think about ways you can step out and take a risk. Ask God for his strength and courage.

- ✿ Get on the dance floor! Just because someone doesn't ask you to dance doesn't mean you can't get your groove on. Don't wait for someone else to do something or to do something with you. If you have a dream or desire, pursue it on your own.

- ✿ Incorporate the *Why not?* risk mentality into a decision you make this week.

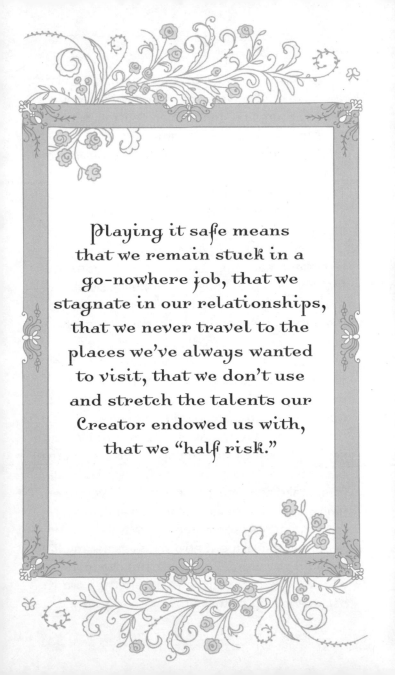

Playing it safe means
that we remain stuck in a
go-nowhere job, that we
stagnate in our relationships,
that we never travel to the
places we've always wanted
to visit, that we don't use
and stretch the talents our
Creator endowed us with,
that we "half risk."

[1] In some versions of the fairy tale, Dad is still alive—but a whipped man whose second wife, Cinderella's stepmother, controls him.

[2] To read more of her amazing story, check out her book, *Until We All Come Home* (FaithWords, 2012).

[3] Names have been changed.

[4] Name and some details have been changed.

[5] Let me be clear about something regarding marriage. If you're in a relationship that involves real abuse or infidelity, by all means, you are free to leave it. However, a majority of the people I've encountered who have gotten divorced did so out of a self-centered, self-motivated decision—and none of them found that their decision brought them lasting, God-honoring happiness. If you feel that your marriage is in a hopeless place, I *urge* you to take the risk to do everything you can to make it better. Get some wise, objective counsel (not from your mama), pray, *fast*, talk, listen, take an honest assessment of your own faults, and *then* decide. Marriage ain't easy. I have moments (sometimes once a day) when I fleetingly think about how much easier my life would be if I weren't married. But I've made a covenant with my husband before the Lord to *risk everything* to make my marriage work. If

you're married, you did the same. Just sayin'.

[6] Interesting tidbit: when *Dead Poets Society* was released in 1989, it became the tenth biggest grossing film of the year at the US box office, beating out Disney's *The Little Mermaid*. http://www.imdb.com/title/tt0097165/trivia?ref_=tt_trv_trv.

[7] John Keating.

[8] John Keating.

[9] Neil Perry, quoting Henry David Thoreau. This quote actually doesn't come directly from a poem, as the *DPS* script leads you to believe, but rather from Thoreau's work *Where I Lived*, chapter 2; http://www.imdb.com/title/tt0097165/trivia?tab=qt&ref_=tt_trv_qu.

Chapter 6

BEAUTY: LOOKING BEYOND THE BEASTLY SURFACE ("WHAT'S BEHIND ALL THAT HAIR?")

"The Lord does not look at the things people look at. People look at the outward appearance, but the Lord looks at the heart."
1 Samuel 16:7 niv

Bless Belle's heart, she's stuck with a father who isn't the wisest with finances or big hairy beasts.[1] Her dad, a wealthy merchant, loses his shirt and everything else when his goods are tossed in a storm at sea. Forced to move to a farmhouse, Belle and her two sisters must now (gasp!) work for a living. That doesn't bother Belle so much—who is known for her kindness and purity of heart—since her two older, wicked, selfish, and vain sisters have treated her like a servant for years.

Later, when their father's ship comes in again (literally), Belle's sisters are overjoyed. Now they can return to their lives of parading around the neighborhood in Dolce & Gabbana and Prada. So they demand that their father return from his trip to the ship bearing expensive gifts of Gucci bags, Versace gowns, and Tiffany bracelets. When Daddy asks Belle what she desires, she requests simply a rose, since none grow where they live.

The trip is a bust, since the ship indeed came in but all the cargo was seized to cover Daddy's debts. Now truly destitute, he heads home—without his daughters' presents. Refusing to ask directions (insert stereotypical joke here), Dad gets lost and eventually stumbles upon a magnificent estate. After a curiously invisible owner invites him to dine and stay the night, Dad accepts and the next day repays the owner's hospitality by picking a prize rose from the estate's bountiful garden—as a gift for his Belle. Bad move.

The owner, now showing his beastliness, bolts toward the poor merchant and bares his large teeth. "*Rooooaarrrrr*. How dare you take my most precious possession? The one thing I love—and you would steal it from me? I will show you what happens to thieves: you will die!"

The merchant falls to his bone-cracking knees and begs for his life. "I only saw the rose and thought of my daughter. She requested that I bring one to her because we don't have roses in our part of the country and, you see, I'm a mer—"

"Enough!" The Beast paces back and forth, running his paws through his surprisingly well-groomed and magnificent mane. "You may go home and give this daughter of yours *my* rose, but then you must return."

"Of course, of course!" Dad gasps out his promise. Armed with the rose, and a Gucci bag and Chanel perfume—compliments of the Beast—along with clear directions, Dad leaves the castle and heads for home. But upon arriving home, his distress captures the attention of Belle, who pries the story from him ("It was that rose that you wanted that got me into trouble, I tell you. . ."). She vows to return to the castle in place of her father—and *he lets her*.

Upon her arrival at the castle, she is surprised to discover that the Beast is one ugly dude, yes, but he is also incredibly gracious, kind, smart, funny, and practices good hygiene. They talk books and swap hair care tips, and Belle soon realizes that compared to his outward disagreeable physique, his inward kindness is actually quite pleasant. Still, when the Beast asks her to marry him *every night*, she thinks about all the hair in the sink that she would be forced to endure, and she refuses. Finally, she admits that she simply can't marry him because she's too homesick and wants to see her father.

Because the Beast is now in love with the Beauty and wants her to enjoy happiness, he allows her to go. She sets off with two presents that the Beast has given her: an enchanted mirror, so she can see him at any time, and a ring that will magically take her (think *Star Trek*'s transporter) back to the castle when she's ready.

Although Beauty is happy to see her father and her vicious, Prada-clad sisters, she finds that she misses the Beast more than she had anticipated.

Sure, he's Mr. Big and Ugly and has fangs and has to watch out for fleas, she thinks, *but he's always treated me with respect and dignity*.

She pulls out the mirror to see what he's

up to and is horrified to discover that he is lying half-dead and heartbroken. Immediately, she pulls out the ring and returns to the Beast, where she throws herself on him, weeping, and promises to marry him.

Her tears fall upon the Beast and he is transformed into a fetching prince. Eyes wide and disbelieving, Beauty falls back on her heels, momentarily wondering if the ring's transponder has caused her mind to turn to jelly and then wondering if she'd only thought to shave him earlier, she could have avoided all this drama.

Beasty Boy explains that he was the victim of a cruel fairy who placed a curse on him because he refused to let her in from the ravages of rain. Only by finding a woman who would love him for his character and not his looks would he be able to break the curse.

Thrilled by the outcome, the two marry and live happily, and handsomely, ever after.

The Old Adage "You Can't Judge a Book by Its Cover"

I love the story of *Beauty and the Beast*. Mostly because Belle is the first female character that I identify with. Belle loves literature, and I, too, am often found with my nose in a book. I can pass up Macy's, but put me close to a bookstore and the lady goes gaga.

But more than the bibliophile admiration, I love that Belle discovers the truth behind the age-old adage, "You can't judge a book by its cover." The Beast had a, well, beastly cover. And yet his heart, his character, his kindness showed a *New York Times* bestseller storyline. If she'd based her entire judgment on his outward appearance, she would have missed some great bedtime reading opportunities. Beauty's compassion and heart led her to see behind the Mr. Big and Ugly to a person who wanted love and understanding and who wanted to give those in return.

She also holds a mirror to so many of our circumstances: how often do we miss the blessings because we can't get past the things that seem disagreeable to our senses?

The most evident application here, obviously, is regarding our love lives. We want a man who makes us laugh like Kevin Hart, who treats us as if we're Princess Kate, and who respects our emotions as well as our bodies—but only if he also looks like Bradley Cooper.

I have a good friend who struggles with this challenge. She's attractive and funny and finds something wrong (usually physically) with every guy she dates. He's too short, he's too tall, his nose protrudes too much, he has batlike ears, his teeth aren't completely straight, his gut hangs slightly over his belt, his fingernails aren't cut evenly, his eyes are wide-set, his lips are too thin, his chest is too hairy.

I never knew a person could find that many things to avoid getting to know the man behind the bat ears. Now into her fourth decade, she is still single. My fear is that if she finally found the perfect-looking (literally) guy, she'd find something else to be unhappy about.

Granted, the case can be made for those folks who *only* judge the book by its cover. I've met brilliant men whose gorgeous wives couldn't carry on a conversation if you were reciting the alphabet. These men may carry a lovely trophy wife on their arms to show off at cocktail parties and work shindigs, but I bet at home, having a person who isn't compatible gets a mite bit thin on the happiness scale.

But beyond the romantic love application, we miss opportunities to connect with people in regular relationships because of outward issues. We don't sit with the lonely senior citizen in church because she smells. We don't lend a hand to a homeless girl because she's dirty.

A very dear woman I know confessed one time that her childhood was devastating because she was so poor her family didn't know about hygiene. She lived in the backwoods and didn't have running water or toothbrushes or pads. No one would sit with her or befriend her. That happened in the 1940s and '50s and she still carries that pain.

Even the Old Testament prophet Samuel fell victim to outward appearances. The king, Saul, had rebelled against God, and as a consequence, God told Samuel that he was appointing a new king. Samuel was to go to Bethlehem and find a man named Jesse who had many sons. God had decided one of the sons was to be the next king.

So Samuel went to Bethlehem and invited Jesse and his family to a special ceremony to honor God. They came, and as each son passed Samuel—all strong and burly—he thought, *Ah, this is the one.*

Each time, God said no. He told Samuel, "'The Lord does not look at the things people look at. People look at the outward appearance, but the Lord looks at the heart'" (1 Samuel 16:7 NIV).

Instead of choosing the strongest, tallest, most burly warrior to be the great king, God chose a young shepherd boy who loved to play music, write poetry, fling rocks at giants, and who was totally sold out for God.

The point is, we miss out on so many

opportunities to serve, to honor, to love and be loved when we base our judgments foremost on a person's outward appearance or actions. But I know you knew that already.

Give It (or Them) Another Shot

If we want a rich and fulfilling happily-ever-after life, then we have to look beyond first appearances. Not everyone or everything will make an astounding first impression, so we need to lend the opportunity for them to show their more lovely side. Many years ago, I was hired at a company that I had respected and longed to work for. Just getting my foot in the door was a huge deal, and I accepted a job in administration with the hopes that I'd pay my dues and work my way up the career ladder. On my first day, I was given the simple job of typing out envelopes. A no-brainer task I could have done in my sleep, but I didn't care because I was there and I was going to do whatever I could to prove myself worthy of belonging in this organization.

I sat at the typewriter (ahem, the company was not-for-profit and apparently hadn't figured out how to use a computer to address envelopes) and began to type. Envelope after envelope went into the typewriter and came out fully addressed. I was whizzing through and feeling good about it all.

And then Cindy walked into my workspace.

She hovered over my shoulder and announced, rather loudly, "You're doing those wrong. The addresses are supposed to be *all capitalized*. You haven't done that. You'll have to do them all again."

I was crushed. This woman wasn't even my boss. She had exactly the same job—and title—as I held. And anyway, who cared? It wasn't as if the post office would refuse to deliver an envelope addressed to "John Doe" versus "JOHN DOE." And I seriously doubted that the person who received the envelope would look at the address and think, *What's that company's problem? Don't they know the entire address is supposed to be capitalized?*

Immediately, my excitement deflated into dread. *This* was going to be my new job? Enduring this woman who was loud, bossy, and inserted her busy-bodyness into my work?

That night I went home and cried. This wasn't what I'd expected for my job. I wasn't even sure I now wanted the job I'd fought so hard for.

If this is what every day is going to be like,

forget it, I'd thought. *I'll find another career path.*

I was willing to chuck it all—my goals, my dreams, and my livelihood. And after only one day.

But I stuck it out, determined to give her a wide berth and try to stay focused on my goals. Since Cindy was in my department, however, I couldn't completely ignore her, and soon, to my complete shock, I found that I *really* liked her. She was fun, funny, caring, boisterous, and generous. She never knew a stranger. And five years after I met her, she donned a purple bridesmaid dress and walked down the aisle at my wedding.

I can laugh about that first day now. And I'm grateful I stuck it out—not only at the company but with her. If I'd allowed that first impression to rule over me, I'd never have been blessed to have my sweet friend and I might never have moved on and up in the company.

Sometimes we just have to dig down a little beneath the surface with someone to discover why they irritate us so much. Sometimes we simply need to give them another shot.

My Scott is hearing impaired. That drives me crazy because I'm never sure when he can't hear me and when he just ignores me (although he assures me that most of the time it's the former). When he can't hear, though, he doesn't let anyone in on that secret, so it's easy for some people to immediately judge him as being arrogant or uncaring, when the reality is that he just can't hear them. If they talk to him and his back is toward them, he can't hear. If they have a soft voice, he can't hear. He isn't ignoring or being haughty. When I'm with him, I'll either respond or repeat their comment or question so that he can then respond.

I imagine some people would take that first impression and then never dig deeper to discover that Scott is actually the most charming person they'll ever meet. They'll miss his swift and dry humor that makes me laugh so hard that sometimes I snort. They'll fail to discover what an immense heart and concern he has for people and his amazing capacity to offer grace. He is, far and away, one of the greatest people I know. But they may miss all of those wonderful things because they based their entire opinion and judgment on miscues and a lack of knowledge.

Sometimes we need to give people the benefit of another opportunity because they're dealing with some insecurity. When I am intimidated or when I really admire someone, I become stupid. I lose major IQ points and I giggle and don't make a lick of sense. (My father says it's because I'm blond.) Frankly, it's embarrassing—probably as much for the other person as it is for me. That's my insecurity showing up.

While my insecurity makes me a dodo, other people's makes them cold and humorless. I know a woman who is a great lady, but when she feels intimidated, she's snarky and harsh. Without a second chance at getting to know why she is the way she is, we'd never know the great side of her.

Give people another shot. If they fail you, then move on. But what if they don't? What if they turn out to be a huge blessing in your life? Perhaps it's worth the risk of learning either way.

EMBRACING THE HAPPY LIFE:

❀ Is there someone or something that you've written off after a first impression? What if you dug a little deeper to find out why that person is the way he or she is?

❀ Was there a time when you made a terrible impression? How did it make you feel? What can you learn from that experience as you relate to others who are different from you?

WHAT'S IN IT FOR ME?

❀ Not everyone makes a dazzling first impression, so give a person the benefit of the doubt and the opportunity to reveal their more beautiful sides.

❀ Find someone who may be disagreeable in appearance and do something kind for them. Peel back the outward layers and see what treasures lie beneath.

Not everyone or
everything will
make an astounding
first impression,
so we need to lend the
opportunity for them
to show their more
lovely side.

[1] Taken from the traditional French fairy-tale version of *Beauty and the Beast* (*La Belle et la Bête*), written by Jeanne-Marie Leprince de Beaumont in 1756. The Disney retelling is based off this version.

Chapter 7

THE UGLY DUCKLING: LET'S NOT DUCK THOSE SELF-CONFIDENCE ISSUES OR. . .TUNING IN TO YOUR QUACKY SWAN SONG

I praise you because I am fearfully and wonderfully made; your works are wonderful, I know that full well.

PSALM 139:14 NIV

he e-mail caught me by surprise, although if I'd thought much about it, it shouldn't have.

GINGER MCFARLAND KOLBABA!
YOU'RE INVITED TO ATTEND KENMORE HIGH SCHOOL'S
CLASS OF 19xx[1]
TENTH YEAR REUNION.

I leaned back in my chair as a plethora of emotions washed over me. When I graduated from high school, I walked away and never looked back. It wasn't that my high school years were terrible (were anybody's actually really good?), but they had been difficult. Adolescence in all its beastly glory shines for all to see—and to remember. I'd done stupid things (like making a snide comment about my French teacher to a friend who then snitched on me). I'd graduated at the top of my class but still felt as though I wasn't all that smart, cool, pretty, thin, fill-in-the-blank.

Faces flashed across the yearbook pages of my mind. The cliques. The drugheads. The football players. The nerds. The band geeks (that was me). Had time really changed anything? Did I want to go back and make small talk with a bunch of people I wouldn't have anything to do with just a decade before? Did I really want to display all my inadequacies and flab?

I delayed responding to the invitation. Maybe if I avoided it, it would go away. But then an old high school friend contacted me. "Are you going? I think we should go. It'll be fun!"

I finally acquiesced and then immediately went on a diet.

The reunion night came and I shoved myself into the tightest body binders I could find to fit into a cute little green dress. I curled my hair and actually put on makeup. And nerves a-bundle, I drove to the party.

I had the best time! Sure, I enjoyed the fact that many of the clique folks were chunkier and balding, but more so, I realized that they were all in the same boat as I was. They, too, were nervous and feeling insecure. Wanting to impress, to be somebody important, someone who mattered. I also realized that we spend four years in a precursor to hell, and then we spend the rest of our lives trying to overcome it. Can I get an amen?

Here's the truth. I could go and enjoy my high school reunion because *I'm not who I was*. I don't have to live under the dark cloud of the past. I don't have to feel blackmailed by my past choices and words and attitudes. I'm different. And I bet you are, too.

The Ugly Duckling²

The day had finally arrived. The barnyard duck could feel the eggs, which she'd so faithfully sheltered under her, begin to crack. One by one, feathery, fluffy, adorable ducklings broke out into their new world. They waddled around to the amusement and admiration of the other barnyard neighbors. And then the last duckling arrived on the scene. This baby wasn't as feathery, fluffy, or adorable as her siblings. In fact, she was rather plain and clumsy. Her neck was too long and her coloring was off. She was ugly—everybody said so, so it must be the truth.

Tormented by the constant barrage of mean comments and wise quacks, finally even her mother sighed and thought it would be better if Ugly were no longer around. She might have been unattractive, but the young duckling wasn't stupid: she knew when someone didn't want her, so she headed off on her own.

Soon she came upon some wild ducks. Although they were friendly enough, she overheard them exclaim, "She can stay—but I hope she doesn't try to marry into our family.

Can you imagine their children? Ug. Ly."

With more hurt feelings, Ugly Duckling headed off again. This time she found herself by a run-down cabin with a poor old woman, a chicken, and a cat. The woman allowed her to stay—but only if she'd produce eggs.

As hard as she tried, Ugly couldn't.

Great! she cried as she waddled around the yard. *Not only am I hideous, now I'm infertile too.*

Once again, she wandered off alone. Barely surviving the winter, as spring finally came, she stumbled upon a pond covered with lily pads and flowers. But more stunning were the beautiful, graceful birds she saw. They had long necks and pure white feathers and the best posture she'd ever seen.

As she stared in awe, these birds caught sight of her and rushed toward her. Sure that they meant to bully or attack her, Ugly bowed her head, tensing herself for the harsh blows.

But wait a Daffy Duck minute. Ugly caught a glimpse of her reflection in the water. Long neck, pure white feathers, great posture. She was a swan!

The Ugly Duckling's creator, Hans Christian Andersen, finishes his story this way:

> *She was thankful that she had known so much want, and gone through so much suffering, for it made her appreciate her*

present happiness and the loveliness of everything about her all the more. . . .

She thought of the time when she had been mocked and persecuted. And now everyone said that she was the most beautiful of the most beautiful birds. And the lilac bushes stretched their branches right down to the water for her. The sun shone so warm and brightly. She ruffled her feathers and raised her slender neck, while out of the joy in her heart, she thought, **Such happiness I did not dream of when I was the ugly duckling.**[3]

You and I are swans. We have been created to be beautiful, poised, lovely, gentle, graceful. But too often we don't see ourselves that way. We look in the mirror, we look at ourselves, and we think we're the ugly duckling.

Thank God that what we used to be isn't what we always have to be. We may be shaped by our past, but we aren't held in bondage to it. God has created you and me with specific gifts and priceless worth. Why do we struggle so much with accepting what he has given us?

"God, What Were You Thinking?"

In college I had close friends who were poster girls for femininity. They loved wearing dresses; were sweet, gentle, and soft-spoken; and looked great in pink.

I loved my friends. And I envied them.

Everything they were, I wasn't. I felt that I didn't fit the culture's and the church's expectations for how young women should be. For years I'd pray, *God, make me more soft-spoken and sweet. Why do I have to be so loud, opinionated, and stubborn?* I felt out of place and unacceptable—although no one ever said anything to confirm that.

Then about a decade ago I met Mel Birdwell. She shared my sense of humor. She was strong and opinionated—and she was wonderful. One day she let me in on a secret: for years she'd felt out of place and unacceptable because she didn't fit the expectations that so many others had placed on her in the church and culture. And she'd spent many hours asking God why he made her that way.

His answer came to her on September 11, 2001, when her husband, Brian, was severely burned in the Pentagon attack. For long, hard months afterward, as she walked with her husband through more than thirty surgeries, she saw that the way God created her was a gift. Had she been everything she'd earlier desired, she wouldn't have been able to offer the strength that her family and community needed.[4]

God used Mel's story and personality to help me realize that he didn't make a mistake when he sculpted my personality and gifts. He knew they would be different from other women's because he *wanted* them to be! My responsibility is to use them to his glory.

Now I start every morning thanking God for making me the way he did, and asking that he use me as *he* made me to be.

There are days when I still struggle with accepting who I am. But every day I lean into my Creator, remembering 2 Corinthians 12:9: "'My grace is all you need. My power works best in weakness'" (NLT). And with the apostle Paul, I—you too!—can attest, "So now I am glad to boast about my weaknesses, so that the power of Christ can work through me."[5]

I hear your thoughts. *Yeah, yeah, I've heard that stuff since forever.*

We hear the message that we're priceless and a treasure—but we don't comprehend how deep God's love is for us. We don't really grasp how precious he thinks we are. So it's easier to wear the mantle of who we used to be or who others think we are—or who they think we should be. We allow others to determine our happiness and our worth, when that was never their right or their responsibility.

Honestly, it's taken me a long time to get to the point of being able to say, "I'm okay. I'm comfortable with who I am right now, and I'm worthwhile. I'm precious and priceless to God. He. Loves. *Me*." I've wasted so much time staying away from events and people because of my weight or my insecurities or my fear that people wouldn't like me. How many opportunities at happiness have I lost because of that? It's shameful. It's sad. And that warped perspective of myself is a lie.

Have you been there?

Recently I read a news story about a response mega singing sensation Taylor Swift sent to one of her fans who confessed to being an ugly duckling. Caillou was bullied because of his name and appearance. Here's what she told him:

Caillou—
  Hi pal.
  I was really shocked to hear you say that you'd been bullied because of your name because the first thing I thought

when I saw it was "woah, Caillou is such a cool name." Honestly. I thought it was so cool because it's different, and herein lies our issue: you will always be criticized and teased and bullied for things that make you different, but usually those things will be what set you apart. The things that set you apart from the pack, the things that you once thought were your weaknesses will someday become your strengths. So if they say you're weird or annoying or strange or too this or not enough that, maybe it's because you threaten them. Maybe you threaten them because you're not the norm. And if you're not the norm, give yourself a standing ovation.

Now I want to tell you that I think you look great the way you are. No one has the right to criticize you for the way your body looks, but they will. One thing I've learned from experiencing this exact kind of criticism is that no one else can label your body except for you. No one gets to have a place in your mind if they weren't invited there by you. So please do me this one favor: don't let their ugly words into your beautiful mind.[6]

Her words prodded me. How many times have I needed to be reminded of those things? How many times do I believe the lies about who I am, who I've been created uniquely to be, what I believe, what I feel, what I look like, how I think? Those lies that we believe about ourselves rip happiness right out of our grasp.

We must not "cling to an outdated self-image, especially an unflattering one," writes Wendy Paris in "Everything You Should Have Learned about Love from Fairy Tales but Probably Didn't." "Once the formerly 'ugly' duckling realized she was a swan, she didn't obsess about turning back into a duckling. She let her grim past stay where it belonged—behind her—and focused on her new life."[7]

The same goes for Cinderella, I'm sure. Can you imagine her being married to a prince, but instead of embracing her royal position, she insists on continuing to clean the fireplaces and act as though she's a servant? She was no longer a cinder maid. She didn't need to live under the shadow of who she used to be.

Neither do we. We need to embrace who God created us to be. And live it out intentionally.

But They Don't Think I've Changed!

Time for the cold, hard, frustrating reality. Some people will never see you as a changed person. How you were years ago is how they'll continue to see you. You may be a swan, but they'll forever label you as the ugly duckling. "Remember when you were the *ugly* duckling? Yeah, you were really 'fowl.' Hahahaha. Bless your heart."

Your mother is probably one of those folks. Just last week my mom said to me in a surprised voice, "You know, I still see you as a thirteen-year-old." Of every age she could have picked, she went with the junior high years? But then later she admitted, "You have changed. You've matured. You've become kinder and sweeter. You're a good kid." I wanted a digital recorder so that the next time she mothered me about something, I could pull it out and replay it for her. Because I'm sure there *will* be a next time when she'll again treat me as if I'm a thirteen-year-old.

Jenny the Jewel knows what it's like to struggle with how other people view her. She writes:

I was born with Down syndrome over 30 years ago. This makes some things very difficult for me. When I was younger, I spent a lot of time asking God, "Why did you make me with Down syndrome? Why can't I be normal like other people?"

I told Him all the time that I didn't like having Down syndrome. I kept thinking that if only I didn't have Down syndrome I would be happy. I thought that somehow God made a mistake when He made me. My mom and dad always told me they loved me so deeply, and that they could not love me any more, but somehow down deep in my heart I always wondered if they would love me more if I didn't have Down syndrome.

When I was in high school, the kids on the school bus were very mean to me. They laughed at me and mocked me, and they called me all kinds of bad names and told me that even my parents couldn't love me. That hurt me so deeply!

When I got off the school bus in the afternoon, I would be crying. My mom met me at the door, and we would talk and pray every day. She told me that people used to say bad things about

Jesus and call Him names, too, so He understood exactly how I felt.

She told me that real truth is only found in God's Word and not in what other people say about you. She told me that if I could find anywhere in the Bible where God calls me bad names or said I was a mistake, she would pay me $5,000. I spent a lot of time reading in the Bible to find out what God said about me. All the scriptures I found said just the opposite, so I never did get the $5,000![8]

If we want a happily ever after, then we need to focus on who we are—and who we are becoming. Thank God that when we let him do his work in us—uninterrupted—he molds and shapes our character into perfection. And he promises to do that until the moment we take our final, very last, I-really-mean-it-no-more-breathing breath.[9]

But You Don't Know Who I Really Am

"If you only knew who I really was and what I've done, you'd understand why happiness eludes me. I deserve to be unhappy." I read the e-mail from a woman who went on to tell me about some of the mistakes she'd made in her life and how every time she tried to make them right, she would do well for a time and then she'd fail again.

Part of her problem was that she didn't really comprehend who she was in Christ. Her faith was frail, and when times got tough, she avoided running directly to the One—the only one—who could help her succeed, who could help her understand that it isn't hopeless and that she was made to learn from her past, conquer it, and move forward into the grace and mercy that God offers.

I told her that I didn't need to know who she thought she really was. I wanted to know if *she* knew who she really was.

Victor Hugo, author of *Les Misérables*, states the idea of finding happiness in our identity this way: "The supreme happiness of life is the conviction of being loved for yourself, or, more correctly, being loved in spite of yourself." When you are working hard to move on past your former self and someone— including yourself—keeps refreshing your memory of how you used to be, then refresh your memory with this truth: *I'm ever changing into the image of Christ, and sometimes it's a messy process, but the Artist thinks I have a lot of potential. So I don't care what you think, or what my mama thinks, or frankly, what your mama thinks. I'm interested in what God thinks.*

Talk about freeing! You have one individual who ultimately matters in their thoughts of you: God. He tells us that we are his "treasured possession" (Deuteronomy 7:6 NIV), the apple of his eye (Psalm 17:8), fearfully and wonderfully made (Psalm 139:14).

When I get a glimpse of who I really am in God's eyes, then I can believe that Jesus' words are true: "Are not five sparrows sold for two pennies? Yet not one of them is forgotten by God. Indeed, the very hairs of your head are all numbered. Don't be afraid; you are worth more than many sparrows" (Luke 12:6–7 NIV).

I ask God:

When I consider your heavens, the work of your fingers, the moon and the stars, which you have set in place, [who am I] that you are mindful of [me]. . .that you care for [me]?
PSALM 8:3–4 NIV

And God answers:

"I, even I, am he who comforts you. Who are you that you fear mortal men, the sons of men, who are but grass,

*that you forget the L*ORD *your Maker,*
who stretched out the heavens and laid
the foundations of the earth, that you
live in constant terror every day
because of the wrath of the oppressor,
who is bent on destruction? . . .
*For I am the L*ORD *your God,*
who churns up the sea so that its waves
*roar—the L*ORD *Almighty is his name.*
I have put my words in your mouth
and covered you with the shadow of my
hand—I who set the heavens in place,
who laid the foundations of the earth,
and who say to Zion, 'You are my
people.'"
ISAIAH 51:12–13, 15–16 NIV 1984

Let that sink in for a moment. Really sink in.
You are no ugly duckling. No matter what
you've done or who you've been. God is a God
of second and third and four thousand forty-
third chances. He has an abundance of grace
that offers us the freedom to blossom into the
swan; we do not have to be who we were. We
are a new creation because of and in Christ.

The writer of Hebrews reinforces this truth
in a verse that makes me tear up every time I
read it (as I'm doing right now). Quoting God,
he writes, "Their sins and lawless acts I will
remember no more" (Hebrews 10:17 NIV).

Embrace who God created the beautiful
you to be.

EMBRACING THE HAPPY LIFE:

❀ Are you comfortable in your own skin? Why or why not?

❀ What would help you become more comfortable and accepting of your identity?

❀ Are you clinging to an outdated self-image—especially an unflattering one?

❀ Do you ever feel as if you're a mistake? Based on this chapter, how have you discovered that kind of thinking to be a lie?

❀ John 10:10 reminds us that "'the thief comes only to steal and kill and destroy; I have come that they may have life, and have it to the full'" (NIV) In what ways have you seen the evil one try to steal from you?

❀ Do you believe you're special? Not like everybody-gets-a-trophy-because-we're-all-winners special, but really, truly unique? If you don't, why?

WHAT THE BIBLE HAS TO SAY:

- ✿ "Anyone who belongs to Christ is a new person. The past is forgotten, and everything is new" (2 Corinthians 5:17 CEV). In what ways have you seen this to be true in your life?

- ✿ "There is now no condemnation for those who are in Christ Jesus" (Romans 8:1 NIV). If this is true, how does it affect how you view yourself? How you live differently?

WHAT'S IN IT FOR ME?

- ✿ When someone criticizes you, consider the source. If they treat you as though you're subpar, that's their problem. "To a duck," writes Wendy Paris, "swanlike grace looks like gawkiness."[10]

- ✿ Memorize scripture. Fill your mind with the truth of who God says you are and how he feels about you.

- ✿ Stop the *if only* game. *If only* I were . . . That game does nothing to bring you happiness. It will suck you dry as quickly as a famished fourteen-year-old boy will eat every cookie you've just baked. As Jenny the Jewel states: "If I spend my time wishing I were different, I will never get around to doing those things God wants me to do."

❀ Try the alternative mind game: *I don't care who I thought I was. I'm a new creation, being shaped and molded to be like Jesus every single day. God has given me this day—this new moment— to show me that I can live fully and glorify him just the way he made me.*

Thank God that what we used to be isn't what we always have to be. We may be shaped by our past, but we aren't held in bondage to it.

[1] Yeah, like I'm going to tell you.

[2] My apologies to Hans Christian Andersen, who wrote this children's story. He created the ugly duckling as a boy. I've given the duck a gender reassignment.

[3] *A Treasury of Hans Christian Andersen*, translated by Erik Christian Haugaard (New York: Nelson Doubleday, Inc., 1974), 175. Pronouns in this quote have been changed to the feminine.

[4] Read Mel and Brian's seriously powerful and amazing story in *Refined by Fire: A Family's Triumph of Love and Faith*.

[5] Parts of this story originally appeared in *Kyria*. Ginger Kolbaba, "God, What Were You Thinking?" *Kyria,* November/December 2011, http://www.todayschristianwoman.com/articles/2011/novemberdecember-issue/god-what-were-you-thinking.html.

[6] Ellie Woodward, "This Exchange between Taylor Swift and a Bullied Fan Is Perfect," *Buzzfeed,* January 27, 2015, http://www.buzzfeed.com/elliewoodward/this-exchange-between-taylor-swift-and-a-bullied-fan-is-perf#.oawXY8yQ1.

[7] Wendy Paris, "Everything You Should Have Learned about Love from Fairy Tales but Probably Didn't." *Glamour* magazine. February 2002, 165.

8 Jenny the Jewel, "What God Says about Me!" http://www.cbn.com/spirituallife/Devotions/JennyTheJewel.aspx.

9 "I am certain that God, who began the good work within you, will continue his work until it is finally finished on the day when Christ Jesus returns" (Philippians 1:6 NLT).

10 Paris, "Everything You Should Have Learned about Love from Fairy Tales but Probably Didn't."

Chapter 8

SLEEPING BEAUTY: "WAS IT EIGHT HOURS OF SLEEP A NIGHT OR. . . ?"

*For in six days G*OD *made Heaven,
Earth, and sea, and everything in them;
he rested on the seventh day.
Therefore G*OD *blessed the Sabbath day;
he set it apart as a holy day.*

EXODUS 20:11 MSG

f I were a betting woman, I'd guess you need some rest.

We're busy, busy, busy. We have work and families, church and dinners, housework and homework, sick relatives and needy neighbors. Rest is for the weary, the overwhelmed, the sick, the depressed. We'd love to rest, to take it easy (who wouldn't?), but that's only for the rich, the lazy, and the expired. My husband, Scott, always jokes with me that sleep is for the dead—and we'll have plenty of time for rest when we're six feet under.

Apparently, a lot of people agree with him. According to the National Sleep Foundation, most adults need at least seven to nine hours of sleep each night. But most people actually average less than seven hours. In fact, the National Sleep Association reports that half of all women they surveyed say they wake up feeling unrefreshed. And the Barna Group reports that 58 percent of all women say they do not get enough rest.[1] I don't particularly like throwing around statistics, but I thought these would show us how prevalent sleep deprivation is.

When we don't get enough rest, it slows our thinking, compromises our memory, impairs our decision making and reaction times, and makes us irritable, angry, and stressed. It makes us more likely to have a car accident, become obese, and suffer from diabetes and heart disease. And worse (as if it could get worse), it increases the chances of us suffering from depression.

Feel free to take a nap before you read on.

A University of North Texas study found that people with insomnia and poor sleeping habits are almost ten times more likely to suffer from clinical depression and more than seventeen times more likely to be affected by "clinically significant" anxiety.[2]

When we're tired, unrested, and overscheduled, we become our own worst nightmare: we make ourselves unhappy.

Many people rest only when they're forced into it. Just look at Sleeping Beauty.

Unbeknownst to this sweet-natured sixteen-year-old, she carried a curse from a grumpy fairy who cast a spell that one day she would prick her finger and die. Fortunately, a kinder fairy tried to reverse the enchantment so that the young princess would sleep instead of die. Sure enough, one day the teenager wandered through the castle, saw an old woman at a spindle, and wanted to try it out. And of course, she pricked her finger (because we saw that coming) and fell into a sleep for a hundred years. That's some serious REM sleep.

I've had moments when I've been so overwhelmed that I wished I could simply prick my finger and fall asleep. No one to bother me, no obligations except to dream sweet dreams. Doesn't that sound wonderful? Of course, I'd miss *Downton Abbey*, but I'm sure Netflix will still be around in a century.

Sleeping Beauty was forced to rest. But here's something I bet you didn't know: you and I have been invited into rest.

Permission to Be Lazy

God actually created us to live in a rhythm—we work, we rest, we work, we rest. The Israelites practiced this rhythm by working from sunup to sundown and then resting from sundown to sunup. With work finished for the day, the rest of the time was theirs to do with as they wanted. They focused on God, others, and relaxation. This is something we can practice every day—after all, it's something that God says is holy. In fact, rest is the first thing God called holy (see Genesis 2:3). My friend Brenda says that trying to practice the rhythm of life that God created (work-rest-work-rest) without rest is "like a clanging cymbal in our ears—and in God's."[3]

So God offers us an opportunity *every day*

to rest. But even better, he gives us an entire day every week as well.

When I was growing up, Sunday was a day distinct from all the other days of the week. For one thing—none of the stores were open. My family and I would go to church, then come home and have a nice meal. Then basically we'd just hang out. I'd read or listen to music or take a nap. It was slower, quieter. More relaxing.

When I became an adult, Sundays became church, then errands and e-mail and laundry and work preparing for the next work week. Whatever I couldn't squeeze in on the other days fell to Sunday. By Sunday evening I'd drop into bed, dreading the start to the workweek and having to jump up and do it all over again. I never took a day off. I didn't have the time. And no one I knew did either.

Our culture pressures us to be productive 24-7. Nothing encourages us to stop: not our culture, not our families, not even our churches. Instead, everyone tells us to go, go, go. And we pass that always-on-the-go mentality to our significant others, our friends, and even our children. One friend has her four-year-old daughter in ballet, tap, swimming, drawing, gymnastics, piano, and preschool. Every weekend my friend drags her daughter to different activities with other four-year-olds and their overly scheduled moms.

Recently she confessed that she thinks her daughter might have ADHD.

Ya think? I wanted to tell her and then clunk her upside the head. Four-year-olds do not need to carry phones and planners to keep up with all their activities.

We're so busy, somehow believing that will bring satisfaction. I can tell you from experience, being busy doesn't equal being content. It brings anxiety and a constant wired feeling. When I'm that busy, even when I do take a break to rest, I'm uneasy and on edge— because I have things to do. And when I'm resting, I'm not getting them done. So I may rest, but then I sleep a little less (both from insomnia over worrying that I'm not getting everything done and from choosing to sleep less to try to cram in a little more work). But then I'm tired, so I caffeinate and sugar myself up for the spikes of energy. It's a vicious cycle.

God has something to say about our schedules. He thinks rest is so important for us to function well and to feel contented that he made it one of the big Ten (as in commandments). In Exodus 20, God tells his people: "Work six days and do everything you need to do. But the seventh day is a Sabbath to GOD, your God. Don't do any work. . . For in six days GOD made Heaven, Earth, and sea, and everything in them; he rested on the seventh day. Therefore God blessed the Sabbath day; he set it apart as a holy day" (Exodus 20:9–11 MSG).

God wants us to unplug completely and do no work. The word *Sabbath* literally means stop, pause, cease, desist. He has commanded us to take a whole day *every week* to rejuvenate ourselves. Or as I like to say: God *wants* us to be lazy! Isn't that the greatest command ever? For one day, God has given you and me permission to do whatever we want—as long as it isn't work related.

You want to take a nap? Go for it!

You want to read that novel that's been sitting on your bed stand collecting dust? Now's your chance!

You want to put together a jigsaw puzzle? Yes!

Many years ago, some friends and I floated down a slow-moving river on inner tubes. My hands grazed the water as I lazily passed through God's nature. To this day, it's still one of my best times of rejuvenation.

Whatever brings you joy and satisfies your spirit is exactly what God desires for you to pursue. And I can guarantee doing laundry and balancing your finances doesn't fall in that category.

What Keeps Us from Enjoying Rest?

What's interesting is that too often we break that commandment—and brag about it. I've been in conversations where we complain about all the work we have to do and how we don't have time to take off. Of course, we don't brag about breaking the other commandments: "I'm planning to steal something." Or, "I think I'll take God's name in vain." Or, "I'm going to go commit adultery."

Maybe we break the Sabbath commandment because we're more comfortable with working than with stopping? Maybe we use the excuse that we have too many kids, too many responsibilities, too many whatevers to actually really obey that particular command. Maybe because honoring the Sabbath requires a humility—an acknowledgment that we aren't willing to admit? *God rested after his work, but I'm exempt. I just have too much to do.*

The reality is, as Keri Wyatt Kent says, we have all the time to do the things that God has called us to do. "We feel, *That's impossible. I do not have all the time I need*. You don't. You have all the time you need to do the things that *God* has called you to do. . . . People ask, 'How am I ever going to get everything done if I take a full day off?' It's one of those mysterious paradoxes: resting makes you more efficient. I get so much done on Mondays because I'm refueled."[4]

The wonderful thing is that God made us to need rest—but also to enjoy it. He wouldn't command us to do something that doesn't fit who or what we are. God didn't make our bodies to go nonstop. He wants us to refuel—and to refocus; to remember that God is in charge. He's got everything handled and we can let go.

What if we started to look at Sabbath rest as an outrageous gift God has given you and me every seven days? Do you think if we trust him enough with our schedules, he'll bless us by giving us freedom, delight, and true worship? Rest and play?

There's a great line in *The Lord of the Rings*. Tolkien writes, "The future, good or ill, was not forgotten, but ceased to have power over the present." That's the promise and joy of celebrating Sabbath. That's what I want to intentionally go after. How about you?

So What Do I *Do* When I Rest?

Taking an entire day to refuel our spirits and souls may sound wonderful, but to a lot of people it can actually strike fear into their hearts. *What do I do for a whole day?* they wonder frantically. Therein lies the rub: we're so used to going that we bring that mind-set into our rest. God tells us to go for six days, but for the seventh day, we are simply to *be*. For some people that's like asking them to turn into a zombie!

In *The Rest of God*, Mark Buchanan offers two suggestions for how to approach Sabbath rest: "Cease from what is necessary" and "embrace that which gives life."[5]

CEASE FROM WHAT IS NECESSARY.

Take a quick inventory of your life and schedule. Thinking about ceasing what is necessary, make a list of what that would look like for you. Nancy Beach suggests these ideas as a jumping-off point:

> We cease from:[6]
> ❧ Work (and thinking about work!). That includes our outside jobs and our domestic ones.

- ❀ Physical exhaustion

- ❀ Hurry

- ❀ Multitasking

- ❀ Competitiveness

- ❀ Worry. For one day, refuse to allow worry a place in your mental space.

- ❀ Decision making

- ❀ Errands

- ❀ Technology. Yep, put down the phone. Give up the social media. Really and truly unplug.

- ❀ Shopping. You may think that's energizing, but it ain't.

Imagine if you stopped multitasking. How would that affect your relationships? All of a sudden, Mom gives undivided attention to her kids who want to talk with her. Husband gets a wife who isn't so distracted. What are the things that you could cease from?

EMBRACE THAT WHICH GIVES LIFE.

Take heart, the above list isn't meant to make you panic. Sabbath is really about freedom. If you don't have to vacuum, what could you do instead that would bring you delight? What would make you appreciate the day and realize what a good gift God gave you?

One of the best ways to embrace the day is to start it through worship. If we want true joy and rejuvenation, we must first go to the Giver of life—the One who presented us with the gift of rest and happiness. Attend a worship service, pray, sing songs that praise and honor God. Reflect on God's goodness to us and how he works in and through our lives. And for goodness' sake, play! Get outside. Take a walk or ride your bike and enjoy God's creation. Laugh heartily. If you're married, make love. (I have a Jewish friend who told me that you get extra holy points if you have married sex on the Sabbath. Who knew?)

Let the dishes pile up. Allow yourself even to feel boredom. But practice the gift of rest.

"If we desire to celebrate God's sovereignty and provision," writes Carolyn Arends, "if we want to live as if we truly believe that all things live and move and have their being in Christ (rather than in our management skills), we may have to consider the spiritual practices of snowboarding, Scrabble, or sand castle building. We may need, as Jesus so famously suggested,[7] to become like children again."[8]

Be Intentional

You and I both know that rest doesn't just happen. Nature hates a vacuum, so if we cease from doing what is necessary, we must fill it with something, or something will come along to fill it for us. That's why we must be intentional in pursuing rest.

Unless you have the same Sleeping Beauty enchantment and are afraid of pricking your finger, you won't casually slide into practicing and enjoying rest. It requires humility and trust. We have to believe that the world will continue to run without our input for one day, and we trust that God has got it all under control.

Being intentional doesn't mean becoming legalistic, however. If you're married and have eight kids and decide you're going to incorporate Sabbath into your week, it's probably best to start slowly. Let those around you know that you're going to start making some changes in order for you to become a better person—who would fight someone on that strategy? But stick to it. If you say that part of your Sabbath rest includes no shopping, then stand firm but kind when your teenage daughter wants to go to the mall to buy a new outfit. Simply remind her that you've chosen not to participate in shopping on this one day of the week.

As you make Sabbath rest a habit, preparation becomes more ingrained. I know one woman who spends the day before running errands and cooking for Sabbath. Then on her "day off," everyone warms up their food and eats. God even thought that was a good idea: in the wilderness, he provided the Hebrew people with extra manna and quail the day before the Sabbath so they didn't have to go out and gather it on their day of rest.

The point is that it's supposed to be simple.

But No One Else Wants to Let Me Rest!

Your son Jamie has soccer practice on Sundays and your daughter Sarah has to work at the mall. And you've decided to practice Sabbath. Smackdown!

Not really, although those can be real concerns. While it may be tempting to use those circumstances to avoid resting, be careful not to let your needs get squeezed out by others' demands. Maybe for your situation, it isn't cold turkey. Maybe it's taking a portion of the day and adding hours. Maybe it's starting with a smaller list of things to be free from and then allowing it to grow as your family gets used to your decisions—and they see that you stand firm with them.

What's important is that you communicate what you're planning. Give your family and friends some idea of what those Sabbath days are going to look like. Slow dinners around the dinner table. Playing games. Going for walks. Uninterrupted and undivided attention. Naps. Hot baths. Manis and pedis. Reading. Praying. Meditating. List all the wonderful things you're going to allow yourself to do.

And then let them know what Sabbath rest won't include for you. Make sure you communicate clearly, so that when someone gets frustrated or when they forget, you'll gently remind them that tomorrow is another day and you'll be more than happy to help them out *then*.

Also consider how you want to count the day. Do you want to go from sunup to sunup? Or practice as the Jews do: from sunset to sunset? They start Friday evening, generally with lighting candles (to remind them that this day is set apart), and then they enjoy a slow meal with good fellowship. They get a full night's sleep and attend synagogue services.

After the next sundown, they go back to focus on the week's schedule and prep for it.

As your family begins to see your commitment—and the wonderful results of a happier, healthier you—they may get on board or they may not. But you choose for you. If you have younger children, it's much easier to determine that all of you are going to follow this day of rest. That teaches your kids the power of rest and the importance of stopping to focus on God and his blessings.

"Start with yourself—the only person you have the power to change," Keri Wyatt Kent suggests. "Gradually cut more tasks; aim for being a calm presence in your family. See if you can change enough that they notice without you saying anything.

"After a month or more of changing only you, tell your family what you're doing, and set a boundary. You might say, 'I'm trying to slow down my Sundays and make them a day of rest, as the Bible commands. I'd love for you to join me. The next step in this process for me is to not run errands on that day, even for a school assignment.' (Give them advance warning.)" [9]

The truth is that you can practice without anyone else joining you. Your happiness doesn't depend on someone else. It depends on what you decide.

Several years ago, I overheard a woman talking about incorporating Sabbath into her weekly schedule. The other woman snorted and said, "Yeah, well, it's not as easy when you have kids. You're single. But when you get a kid, let me know how that rest theory works for you."

Harsh words.

But the truth is that if you're single, if you're a mom of a toddler, if you're a mom of nine kids—it doesn't matter. That fourth commandment doesn't have a disclaimer that says, "You can opt out of Sabbath rest if you fall under any of the following circumstances. . ."

Here's another reality: kids are the absolute best at modeling Sabbath rest. They play, they laugh, they run, they nap, they get up and play some more—and they don't work. I think they understand that commandment a whole lot better than we do!

But I Feel So Guilty!

I remember when I first decided to practice Sabbath more intentionally, I talked to my husband about my need for rest and how I felt that if I obeyed God in this commandment I would actually become more productive and be a kinder wife. Although I was disappointed that he opted not to join me, I stayed firm in my decision.

That was difficult because the guilt overwhelmed me. As I watched him doing things around the house, which I would normally help him do, I struggled not to get up and start working. But I forced myself to remain seated on the couch with a novel.

Lazy! my mind tried to condemn me. *You should feel guilty. Look at him working while you sit there as though you don't have a care in the world. You're making him cook his own dinner? What kind of wife are you?*

The barrage of thoughts pounded me over and over. So I began to compromise with my brain: *Well, maybe if I did just a little bit—I could still rest later. A little rest is better than no rest, right?*

But then another voice whispered, *No work. Enjoy this day of freedom. If your husband chooses not to join you, then he's accountable for that. Not you.*

Then I began to wonder about including him in my Sabbath rest—but doing it without him realizing what I was doing. "Hey, babe, do you want to take a walk? It's so pretty out today, let's make the most of the sunshine." Most of the time it worked. But the times that he continued with his to-do list, I had to let it go. I spent time praying and reflecting over how wonderful it would be for Scott to enjoy Sabbath rest, too.

Eventually he joined me. We aren't perfect at practicing Sabbath, but we work at being more intentional about it. And I've noticed that when we do, I discover the next day comes and I have a lot more energy and am excited to start my day.

"Rest. Don't rest. It's up to you ultimately," my friend Eileen told me. "If you choose to go it as a renegade, don't be surprised when lasting happiness eludes you."

Brenda didn't feel as guilty about taking a Sabbath; she just didn't see it as something that she really needed. But she tried it out of obedience.

My journey into rest began more than 20 years ago, and it's been a roller coaster. Acting out of sheer obedience to the Fourth Commandment (once I swallowed hard and admitted I'd been neglecting it my entire life), I moved into Sabbath-keeping kicking and screaming. It was, for many years, the worst day of my week. Having derived my value as a human being from what I could efficiently accomplish in any given day, I had no idea how to let down and relax.[10]

Soon, however, as she remained committed to it, she began to see rest as "a gift to be unwrapped, not a fate to endure."[11]

Getting Started

The first way I'd encourage you to start resting is to make sure you get enough sleep—which is something you don't need to wait until Sabbath to do! Try this treasure every night. Go to bed a little earlier, avoid looking at a lit screen before bed (which can also cause insomnia because it throws off our sleep rhythms), and stay away from caffeine. I discovered that caffeine doesn't affect me as much as sugar does. So I stopped eating sugar after a certain hour.

Take whatever time you can every day to build some rest into your schedule. Even if it's an hour—even if it's locking yourself in the bathroom for fifteen minutes! Ask another mom to take your kids for an hour so you can rest. And then return the favor. Also, make a point of taking care of your body. Take a walk.

Get moving. Studies show that even simple exercise affects our mood.

Then make a commitment to practice Sabbath. Keri Wyatt Kent started her Sabbath practice by making little changes. Her kids were young, and she desperately wanted a day off, but Sundays were busy days since her husband was a realtor and often had house showings then. Often she'd have to pick a different day as her Sabbath.

But she stuck to it, and as her family's Sabbath time evolved, she noticed that she had become calmer. "I easily get flustered, but I gave myself permission to lighten up," she says. "One Sabbath my daughter and I just watched the squirrels play outside. That may not seem spiritual, but it is."[12]

Now when I get too busy, I pray, *Lord, slow me down. Help me to value rest and spending time with you more than simply accomplishing more. Help me to find the sacred in the ordinary and to find joy in the commonplace. Most of all, help me to focus on you. Help me to find joy in you during this Sabbath time. Take away the sense of duty and make me giddy with the privilege and satisfaction of being with you.* I find it helps me calm down and refocus my priorities.

Let go of being in charge and see what God lays in your path. Make rest an adventure.

And I bet this is what you'll discover: happiness will come, peace and calm will reign, and you'll be a totally different person. But there's something else: you'll discover that God loves you not for what you do, but for who you are. Keri explains, "I'm a doer, and I can believe that God loves me based on what I do. But when I don't accomplish *anything*—and realize God's love is still there, that's when I understand that God's love is unconditional. I'm not sure I'd truly know that if I wasn't practicing Sabbath."[13]

Rest is a wonderful thing and God invites you into it. Just ask the 116-year-old Sleeping Beauty. She got her prince because of it.

EMBRACING THE HAPPY LIFE:

❧ Ask God to open your eyes to the way you spend your time throughout the week. What things could you move around to get some rest?

❧ In what ways could you prepare to begin Sabbath-keeping?

❧ What feels like work to you? Would it be possible to cease doing those things for one day a week? If not, why?

❧ What would you do if all your work was done? If every item on your to-do list was checked off, what would you love to do?

❧ Henry Ward Beecher stated, "A world without a Sabbath would be like a man without a smile, like a summer without flowers, and like a homestead without a garden. It is the most joyous day of the whole week." Are Beecher's words true of you? Why or why not?

❧ In Deuteronomy 5:15, God reminds the Israelites that they were once slaves but now they are free. Slaves don't get a day off. What does that aspect of the Sabbath mean for you today?

❧ Was Sabbath a part of your weekly

ritual growing up? What did your Sabbath ritual look like?

❧ In today's culture we're constantly told to take time for ourselves. How does this cultural mantra coincide with the biblical commandment of Sabbath? In what ways does it differ?

WHAT THE BIBLE HAS TO SAY:

❧ "In peace I will lie down and sleep, for you alone, O Lᴏʀᴅ, will keep me safe" (Psalm 4:8 ɴʟᴛ).

❧ "It is useless for you to work so hard from early morning until late at night, anxiously working for food to eat; for God gives rest to his loved ones" (Psalm 127:2 ɴʟᴛ).

❧ "You can go to bed without fear; you will lie down and sleep soundly. You need not be afraid of sudden disaster or the destruction that comes upon the wicked, for the Lᴏʀᴅ is your security" (Proverbs 3:24–26 ɴʟᴛ).

WHAT OTHERS SAY:

❧ "The happiness of heaven is the constant keeping of the Sabbath.

Heaven is called a Sabbath, to make those who have Sabbaths long for heaven, and those who long for heaven love Sabbaths."—Philip Henry

WHAT'S IN IT FOR ME?

- ✿ What would it take for you to set aside an entire twenty-four hours for a Sabbath? What would you need to get rid of and what would you need to change? Decide on one action to move toward this goal.

- ✿ Play is an essential component of Sabbath. So ask yourself these questions: What do I like to do for fun? What's rejuvenating and enjoyable? What activity, when I do it, causes me to forget about my stress and lose track of time? Then be intentional about incorporating those things into your Sabbath.

- ✿ This week, try intentionally reflecting on what you experience on the Sabbath, remembering what God showed you, and welcoming his ongoing shaping of you.

- ✿ In order to accomplish all your work, you'll probably need help. Get family members involved! Explain to your family that you'd like to take a day off. But that means you need their help. Delegate tasks and chores so that everyone can enjoy and rest on the Sabbath.

✤ Make a list of the things you need to accomplish this week and when you will complete each thing in order to protect this week's Sabbath.

NEED SOME IDEA STARTERS?

✤ Spontaneously play with your kids, even if it means crawling around the house and getting dog hair all over you.

✤ Take a long, hot bath.

✤ Sit on your porch or find a rocking chair and rock yourself.

✤ Go to a playground and swing or slide down the slide.

✤ Read poetry.

✤ Bake bread—but don't clean up the mess.

✤ Sketch.

✤ Journal.

✤ Pray.

✤ Read scripture slowly—just a verse or two.

- ❧ Sit alone in silence.

- ❧ Give yourself a mental break—no obsessing about the way you look.

God wants us to refuel—
and to refocus; to
remember that God
is in charge. He's got
everything handled
and we can let go.

NOTES: CHAPTER 8

1 "Tired & Stressed, but Satisfied: Moms Juggle Kids, Career & Identity." *Barna Group*, May 6, 2014, https://www.barna.org/barna-update/family-kids/669-tired-stressed-but-satisfied-moms-juggle-kids-career-identity#.VM_8Rrk5CUk.

2 Taylor DJ, Lichstein KL, Durrence HH, Reidel BW, Bush AJ. "Epidemiology of Insomnia, Depression, and Anxiety," *PubMed*, 2005, http://www.ncbi.nlm.nih.gov/pubmed/16335332.

3 Brenda Jank, "Public Enemy #1," *Today's Christian Woman*, January 2013, http://www.todayschristianwoman.com/articles/2013/january/public-enemy-1.html.

4 From an interview I had with Keri Wyatt Kent. "Life-Giving Force," *Kyria*, May/June 2011, http://www.todayschristianwoman.com/articles/2011/mayjune-issue/life-giving-force.html.

5 Mark Buchanan, *The Rest of God* (Nashville: Thomas Nelson, 2006), 129.

6 Nancy Beach, "Restore Your Soul," *Kyria,* May/June 2011, http://www.todayschristianwoman.com/articles/2011/mayjune-issue/restore-your-soul.html.

7 See Matthew 18:3.

[8] Carolyn Arends, "Lord, Teach Us to Play," *Kyria*, May/June 2011, http://www.todayschristianwoman.com/articles/2011/mayjune-issue/lord-teach-us-play.html.

[9] "Life-Giving Force."

[10] Jank, "Public Enemy #1."

[11] Ibid.

[12] "Life-Giving Force."

[13] Ibid.

Chapter 9

RAPUNZEL: GIVING UP THE THING THAT HAUNTS US ("HEY, WHAT ARE YOU DOING WITH THOSE SCISSORS?")

"The Lord gave, and the Lord has taken away; blessed be the name of the Lord"

Job 1:21 esv

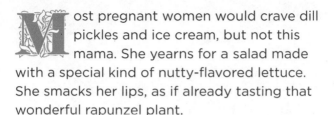ost pregnant women would crave dill pickles and ice cream, but not this mama. She yearns for a salad made with a special kind of nutty-flavored lettuce. She smacks her lips, as if already tasting that wonderful rapunzel plant.

"Husband!" she roars. "Get me some rapunzel or I shall die!"

"Oh, dearest," her husband says as he wrings his hands, for where shall he ever find such a plant, since they stopped carrying it in the local grocery store? "Wouldn't some Nutella work just as well? How about a nice peanut butter and jelly sandwich? A cobb salad? Eggplant?"

"I must have rapunzel!"

"But, sweetheart—"

"I'm carrying this child, and all I ask you to do is make me a salad!"

How can he explain that he knows only one place to get the coveted greens, and it will surely bring trouble upon their house? But as his wife persists, he finally agrees. That night, he climbs the wall surrounding his next-door neighbor's garden. His neighbor, of course, happens to be a witch. He succeeds in gathering the rapunzel plant and heads home, much to his wife's delight. Too much.

The next night she insists on an encore salad, and again he scales the walls. Only this time, Ms. Witchy Witch is ready for him. Caught leafy handed, he begs for mercy.

With a sly smile she agrees to be lenient—on one condition: she gets the baby when it's born. Desperate and in despair, he agrees, vowing never to let his wife forget that she should have accepted the PB&J when it was offered.

A baby girl is born, and the witch raises her as her own. Witchy Mama calls the baby Rapunzel, after the leaf that her birth mother had craved.

As Rapunzel grows into a beautiful young girl with flowing, fair locks, Witchy Mama carries her off to a tower and shuts her away. She is forced to live in the penthouse room with no stairs, no door, no Internet, not even cool posters to cover her wall. There's only one way to enter and exit that tower: through the window. Fortunately, Rapunzel has really long hair.

"Rapunzel, Rapunzel, let down your hair, so that I may climb the golden stair," her adoptive mother calls out whenever she comes for a visit.

Obedient Rapunzel lowers her locks so that the witch can climb up.

Years go by and one day while Rapunzel is alone in the tower, a prince passes through the forest and hears an ethereal voice. Having nothing else to do, Rapunzel spends her days singing show tunes—mostly from the musicals *Hairspray* and *Wicked,* but she also throws in some music from a little-known movie called *Tangled*. Enraptured by her voice, the prince hunts her down and, finding he cannot get to the girl, returns every day just to listen. Finally, he spies Witchy Mama and discovers the secret to the tower's entrance.

He begs Rapunzel to let him up, which she does, and after many such visits, they fall in love and agree to marry. Unfortunately, the witch discovers the plan, cuts off Rapunzel's beautiful and utilitarian hair, and pitches her, without shampoo or conditioner or even a little sculpting gel, into the wild forest to fend for herself.

Later that night when the prince shows up, the witch tricks him and sends down the hair. But instead of Rapunzel, he finds the witch. With no way out and horrified by what his future mother-in-law has done, he throws himself from the tower and falls on some thorns, which blind him.

He wanders through the countryside, because how *would* he find his way home without eyes? Eventually he hears that magical voice, singing "Nobody Knows the Trouble I've Seen," and instantly recognizes that it belongs to his beloved, fair—but now cropped—haired beauty, Rapunzel. Feeling his way toward the voice, he finally reaches the damsel in distress. They embrace, and in their grief, her tears begin to fall over him. Magically, her tears have healing power and his sight is restored. They marry, move into a ranch house with lots of doors and windows, and live happily ever after.

Losing the Things We Love

What a depressing story. Rapunzel never knows her birth parents and is forced to live alone in a dark and dank tower in the middle of nowhere. When she finally meets Prince Charming, she gets kicked out of her home and loses her man and the opportunity for love and marriage. And she loses the thing that's become most dear to her: her hair, which promises escape, a life of freedom way beyond the walls of the high tower, and a nice write-up in *Guinness World Records*.

We've been there (except my hair never got that long): we've lost something dear to us. We've been betrayed. We've been ignored. We've lost love. We've lost opportunities to experience and fulfill our dreams. Whatever that thing was, we didn't ask to lose it. We don't deserve it. We don't like it. And frankly, it really messes up the whole happiness thing.

It affects us deeply. We may become cautious, skeptical, even bitter. In order to cope, we may even force it into our subconscious and go on with life, but it doesn't really go away. And so, in some ways we're the walking wounded, the living dead.

Everyone has scars and suffers loss. Some more than others, but loss visits us all—even the people we think have it all together.

A few years ago, I got together with some college friends whom I adore and whom I hadn't seen for years. These women are amazing. And when I compare myself to them, I always come in just behind them. They make me want to be better, stronger, gentler, kinder. They have always appeared to have everything together. No wounds, no scars, no loss.

But over our weekend time together, we experienced the messy, lovely world of real community. One by one we shared heartaches: depression, a mother's death, job loss, infertility, disease, divorce, unrealized dreams, diets that never lead to weight loss. I was stunned (though I'm not sure why I should have been!) that while they appear to have perfect lives, the truth is that their lives are anything but.

As I sat and listened to each person's heartache, while different from my own, I still felt a deep sense of comfort because I am not alone in my suffering. Others may look put together, but they experience hurt and loss just as I do.

Why Me?

"Why me?"

We've heard people say this in response to a real or perceived tragedy. "Why did this happen to me? Why did God allow this?"

I've been prone to ask these questions on occasion. When my father was diagnosed with cancer, I questioned God, "Why him? He's such a good man." When a good friend was laid off, I wondered, *Why her?* And when I've attended countless baby showers without a hoped-for pregnancy of my own, I've asked, "Why me?"

But the older I get, the more I realize that's the wrong question to ask.

"Why me?" questions never get fully and satisfactorily answered. And if someone offers some lame excuse, it fails to bring comfort because it's just that: a lame excuse. Or worse, a platitude.

Many years ago while my husband and I were building a house, our construction guy dropped his insurance in the middle of the project. We talked with him about renewing it, which he promised to do, but in the meantime, one of his workers fell two stories on our worksite and crushed his leg. (We found out later that he had been shot in that leg and had no feeling, so when he was working on the second floor of the house, he backed up but was unable to sense that he was backing up onto air, and fell.)

The construction owner skipped town, leaving us wide open for a lawsuit. And boy, did we get one. We almost lost everything.

I'd shared the story with a friend at work, who then kindly and disrespectfully shared it with one of her coworkers, a woman who was not on my most-favorite list. One day, she stopped me in the hall and asked about the lawsuit. I was surprised by her question and responded that it was still ongoing. And this was her response:

"Well, you must not have learned yet what God wants you to learn. Otherwise, you wouldn't still be dealing with it."

And then she haughtily went on her way, leaving me in a wake of anger and frustration.

Even though I hadn't officially asked the *why* question, she'd decided to answer it. And what a lame, uncalled for, and harsh response it was!

Ironically, a few years later, this woman's husband went into the hospital for stomach bypass surgery. It went fatally wrong, and for a while he was in a coma and then he eventually died.

While he lay in a coma, I overheard her struggle repeatedly with the *why* question. Okay, yeah, I'm sure you guessed what I really wanted to say to her. But by that time, I'd matured a bit more and wisely kept my mouth shut. By that time, I'd learned what *why* questions really are.

The *why* question has, at its heart, a self-centered, self-protective, tight-fisted focus. We're shocked when troubles burst into our lives. As though somehow we're so special that we're exempt from the trouble trolley.

I knew a woman who was diagnosed with stage 4 cancer. She spent the remaining days of her earthly life asking God *why, why, why*. Every time I visited her, she would raise that question in some form. And honestly, I refused to address it, because I simply couldn't. If I had said anything to try to address that question or comfort her with some platitude, it would have only brought more pain.

I know this because I tried it once. One time when I visited her in the hospital she kept hysterically asking why God was allowing her to suffer, but in the next breath, she attempted to answer her own *why* questions but was doing so with her own set of platitudes. Back and forth her emotional teeter-totter went, until finally I said, "Think about what you've just said: God is in control, he will never leave you. That should bring you comfort, not such fear, yes?" I wanted to help her see that comfort *was* near.

Her eyes squinted and her mouth pursed as she said, "Well, I'm just more tenderhearted. I always have been. *Some* people are just crusty and hard hearted. They don't have compassion."

With that, I was soundly put in my place. And she continued her barrage of wounded *whys*.

Not to be too snarky here, but *why* questions are never going to lead us to our happily ever after. They only perpetuate the suffering and set us up for a joyless existence.

What's the "Right" Question?

So if "Why me?" is a happiness-evading question, what question should we ask that would offer some answers?

I think the first thing for us to remember is that misery comes to us all. No one is exempt. No, not one.

Take a look at the fairy tales. Many of them were written by the *Brothers Grimm*. Their name alone should give us a clue. Want something more spiritual? Have you read the Bible lately? Can you name one character who had an easy life?

Even Jesus told us, "Don't take these things personally. You're going to have trouble. Expect it" (John 16:33, the Ginger translation). And he certainly knew his share of trouble—he took on the sorrow of the entire world.

But as I've heard it said, never waste a tragedy. I think there's truth to that. It stands to reason that if everyone has troubles, God must have something planned for us through that. One plan may be so we can learn the power and importance of gratitude.

A poster boy for trouble is Job. Just about every misfortune that could happen, happened to Job. He lost his entire family. His home. His wealth. His health. His friends. Even his wife got so tired of the hardship, she begged him to curse God and die. And how did he respond? With authentic gratitude. He struggled, he ached, he grieved, and yet in the midst of all his anguish, he praised God.

"He said, 'Naked I came from my mother's womb, and naked shall I return. The Lord gave, and the Lord has taken away; blessed be the name of the Lord'" (Job 1:21 esv).

The military has a motto: "Do the harder right." It's easy to be grateful when life is good and things are going along nicely. But the harder right means we practice thanking God when everything within us screams out, *Why me?*

I've started to realize the right question isn't "Why me?" but rather "Why *not* me?" Why should *I* be exempt?

The interesting thing about asking that question is that it changes my perspective. My eyes move from myself and my current circumstance to the bigger, broader picture of eternity and how God wants to shape me into the image of Jesus.

I've seen it firsthand with my college friends. Fortunately, their story doesn't end with bemoaning their travails. These amazing women (and this is why I adore them) all were so joyful! Each devastating story was followed by a fierce determination to pursue gratitude and restoration. Each woman laid claim to happiness through her faith—not understanding her loss or making light of it, but truly embracing the God who sees us through the easy times *and* the terrifying ones.

I heard each of them say, along with Job, "The Lord is good *always*. I do not understand why he gives or why he removes, but I know I can trust him. I know that he has my ultimate best in store for me, and so I will bless his name."

That's powerful! And it opens the door wide for healing, for hope, for restoration, for a brighter future, and for happiness to reside within us. We don't have to understand why as long as we understand *who* we belong to: the One who never leaves us alone, never ignores or neglects us, never stops loving us, never stops wanting the best for us—even when we don't feel his presence or his hand at work in and around our lives.

When we embrace the "Why *not* me?" question, not only do we mature in our characters and in our spiritual lives, but we're able to empathize with, love, and care for those with similar troubles.

Don't get me wrong. We don't need to walk around looking for trouble so that we can express our gratitude! But hopefully as we practice doing the "harder right" every day and being thankful for what God has blessed us with, when the troubles *do* come, our natural inclination will become, "Why *not* me? Thank you, God, for this circumstance, too. In the midst of it, help me to honor you and bless others."

How Does Gratitude Come?

It sounds so easy, doesn't it? When troubles come, just praise Jesus!

Sounds more like a platitude than an actual, helpful tip.

How do you express gratitude when a bomb goes off and your soldier husband loses his limbs? When a drunk driver kills your child? When you can't get pregnant? When your home goes into foreclosure? When you can't pay your school loans? When the guy you thought was The One turns out to be The Scum? Where is authentic gratitude then?

Job has a lot to teach us about that. So does David. His guttural cry in Psalm 63 shows his anguish, but also his willingness to trust and to thank.

O God, You are my God; early will I seek You; my soul thirsts for You; my flesh longs for You in a dry and thirsty land where there is no water. So I have looked for You in the sanctuary, to see Your power and Your glory. Because Your lovingkindness is better than life, my lips shall praise You. Thus I will bless

*You while I live; I will lift up my hands in
Your name.*
PSALM 63:1–4 NKJV

Gratitude isn't as simple as "name it and
claim it!" Sometimes gratitude is a struggle.
Sometimes it demands that we offer thanksgiving while our teeth are clamped shut and
our fists are clenched. But the first step is to
be willing—even hesitantly so.

BE WILLING.

Seem impossible? Of course it is! We're
human, and we need a savior for this reason.
The apostle Paul tells us that we can do *all*
things—every last bit—through Christ who
gives us strength (see Philippians 4:13). When
we're tempted to fall into the self-pity and the
bitterness of life's misfortunes, we can honestly
pray, *I'm not feeling this, God. I don't see any
reason to be thankful—and I certainly don't feel
like offering you gratitude. This whole thing
stinks.*

He'll take that—because you're being
honest. He'll nod and say, *"Yes, it does stink.
It's horrible, and I feel your pain."*

And that's the start of gratitude right
there. That God agrees with you in the lousy
circumstance that you experienced. So
through gritted teeth you can say, *Okay, thank*

you that you know this is lousy, that I didn't deserve to have this happen to me.

Baby steps are still steps! And God will honor those and help you take bigger ones.

The next baby step is to continue to pray: *God, help me to see the good that can come from this. Help me to find some small measure of joy and hope. Open my eyes so that I'm on the lookout—and open my heart to the possibilities of something good coming from this.*

Another honest prayer that God will answer.

God never says, *"That thing that happened, let's act as if it didn't. Let's just ignore it."* He wants us to name it. If we aren't honest with him about our real thoughts and feelings, then he can't help us heal. His chest is big enough to handle us beating our fists and saying that it isn't fair, that we're angry and afraid. To acknowledge that it was awful, that we don't understand. That's the first step in faith—and the first step to growing our happiness. We need to include God in the conversation and in our thoughts. Partner up with him. When we bring him on our side by honestly addressing what we think and feel (even when it isn't the "proper" thing), then we have a real shot at moving beyond our pain.

SING.

Yes, you read that correctly: sing. Rapunzel got through a lot of her hardship by singing. So did the American slaves. Their experience was horrid—there's no other way to describe what happened to human beings who were kidnapped, ripped from their homeland and their families, and forced into hard labor, poverty, and oppression. Part of what helped them survive was their songs, called spirituals. They were filled with pain and longing, but also with hope that life would someday be better. That justice would come. They sang songs like these:

"Look Down That Long, Lonesome Road"
"Do, Lord, Remember Me"
"Go, Tell It on the Mountain"
"Lonesome Valley"
"Were You There?"
"He's Got the Whole World in His Hands"
"There Is a Balm in Gilead"
"Lord, I Want to Be a Christian"

Music has a mystical way of bringing us solace, of raising our spirits, of summarizing our beliefs, of helping us to remember the hope we have. It doesn't take away what happened or make it any less tragic, but it does help us cope. Here's what one person wrote when she witnessed American slaves singing: "As we wheeled up the avenue, our numbers ever increasing, the Negroes broke into another song, more joyful than the last, and all clapped hands in unison, when they sang the chorus until the air quivered with melody."[1]

Singing centers us back to what is true. It helps move us toward gratitude and a deep-seated joy. Frederick Douglass, an escaped slave who went on to become a famous social reformer, writer, and speaker, wrote this about his captivity: "We were at times remarkably buoyant, singing hymns and making joyous exclamations, almost as triumphant in their tone as if we had already reached a land of freedom and safety."[2]

Listen to music that brings hope to your spirit, and then join in.

I sing in my car, in the shower, while I'm doing dishes. I sing as much as I can because it really does buoy my soul. One day I found myself absentmindedly singing in the frozen food aisle. I had memorized some scripture set to music, and while looking at frozen broccoli florets, I began to sing, "Do not be anxious about anything, but in every situation, by prayer and petition, with thanksgiving, present your requests to God. And the peace of God, which transcends all understanding, will guard your hearts and your minds in Christ Jesus" (Philippians 4:6–7 NIV). I'm sure my fellow grocery shoppers thought I'd lost my heart and mind, but I didn't care. It was a catchy tune and it was bringing me joy.

Over and over throughout the Bible (especially in Psalms), we read about the power of singing. Go to Biblegateway.com or another Bible website and plug in "sing" and see for yourself how often people sing. Here are a few to get you started:

❁ "Sing to him, sing praise to him; tell of all his wonderful acts" (1 Chronicles 16:9 NIV).

❁ "Let all who take refuge in you be glad; let them ever sing for joy. Spread your protection over them, that those who love your name may rejoice in you" (Psalm 5:11 NIV).

❁ "Sing praises to God, sing praises; sing praises to our King, sing praises" (Psalm 47:6 NIV).

❁ "I will sing of your strength, in the morning I will sing of your love; for you are my fortress, my refuge in times of trouble" (Psalm 59:16 NIV).

❁ "Because you are my help, I sing in the shadow of your wings" (Psalm 63:7 NIV).

❁ "My lips will shout for joy when I sing praise to you—I whom you have delivered" (Psalm 71:23 NIV).

- ❀ "I will sing of the Lord's great love forever; with my mouth I will make your faithfulness known through all generations" (Psalm 89:1 NIV).

- ❀ "Come, let us sing for joy to the Lord; let us shout aloud to the Rock of our salvation" (Psalm 95:1 NIV).

In the midst of their imprisonment and trouble, Paul and Silas didn't ask, "Why me?" Instead, they sang: "About midnight Paul and Silas were praying and singing hymns to God, and the other prisoners were listening to them" (Acts 16:25 NIV).

Even God sings—specifically, over *you*: "The Lord your God is with you, the Mighty Warrior who saves. He will take great delight in you; in his love he will no longer rebuke you, but will rejoice over you with singing" (Zephaniah 3:17 NIV).

I know it sounds crazy, but singing really does work.

CRY.

Rapunzel's tears had magical healing power. As she cried over her prince's blindness, her tears restored his sight. Tears heal.

Back in the seventies, Marlo Thomas and Friends released an album called *Free to Be You and Me*. I think I received it one year for Christmas, and I listened to that LP album until it was warped. One of the songs on it told kids that it was all right to cry, because "crying gets the sad out of you" and it will "make you feel better." I loved that song—mostly because, as a sensitive child, I'd cry over a lot of things. My mom once threatened not to let me watch *Frosty the Snowman* because I cried every time he melted. I'd seen it enough to know that (spoiler alert) he comes back to life in the end. It didn't matter, I still cried because it was sad for him to lose his snow body.

I can cry at a McDonald's commercial. (Some of them are really touching. The whole McDonald's-lets-you-pay-for-food-with-lovin' gets a tear in my eye every time.) And those Olympian backstories? Forget about it. I watch the alpine skiing and the bobsled events with a box of tissues.

But I also cried after my mother-in-law died. I held up well when she actually died (I was there) and at the funeral, but several days afterward, as I sat alone at my computer and worked, ache welled up from the bottom of my gut and gushed from me. My throat burned. My eyes throbbed. And I allowed the tears to flow. Actually, I couldn't stop them once they started. It would have been easier for me to close a gushing fire hydrant. For what seemed like an hour, I sobbed until I had nothing left in me. I was wiped out.

And then a slow calm crept over me and I felt at peace. I was still exhausted, but I was okay.

For many in our culture, crying is a sign of weakness. But Jesus blesses those who cry. In Luke 7, while at a Pharisee's house for supper, a woman of ill repute entered, fell at Jesus' feet, and sobbed. She wept so much that essentially she washed his feet with her tears. He was pleased with her actions and forgave her sins.

We see that Jesus also cried.[3] When he learned that his good friend Lazarus had died, he went to the tomb, and the Bible says simply, "Jesus wept" (John 11:35 KJV). That's one of the most powerful and relatable verses in the entire Bible.

Research has shown that tears offer healing. Our bodies produce different kinds of tears—tears that come because we got a speck of something in our eye; tears that lubricate our eyes to keep them from drying out; and emotional tears. Emotional tears are chemically different from the other types. They contain beta-endorphins, our bodies' natural pain relievers. According to Dr. William Frey, a biochemist and former director of the Dry Eye and Tear Research Center, people feel better after crying because they are "removing, in their tears, chemicals that build up during emotional stress." They help rid our bodies of toxins.[4]

Tears do something else for us: people who cry frequently enjoy better health and are happier. Margaret Crepeau, a professor of nursing at Marquette University, says that "laughter and tears are two inherently natural medicines. We can reduce duress, let out negative feelings, and recharge. They truly are the body's own best resources."[5] Plus according to Alan Wolfelt of the University of Colorado Medical School, "Not only do people feel better after crying, they also look better."[6]

So that red nose and eyes you get after weeping? You thought it was a makeup nightmare? Nah, it's a rosy blush!

An Invitation to Let Go

Often one of the most difficult things for us to do when we've suffered deeply is to let it go. Release its hold and power over us. That's scary to do. It requires sacrifice and a trust that God will make right what we've lost. Finding happiness in the midst of deep pain is not a fairy tale. So I don't want you to think I'm offering some platitude that we just "give it to God" (although there is biblical truth in that statement). I'm suggesting that, in some pain, we can grasp gratitude and happiness. And in some, we wait for God to slowly cover us with it.

Several years ago, in one year I knew seven people who died. I watched almost a dozen friends and associates lose their jobs. And I walked with two people who fought cancer. One day as I sat and filled out a sympathy card for another friend who recently lost her husband, I thought about the words I wrote to her: "May you be surrounded by God's tangible presence and feel overwhelmed by his peace and comfort. May you somehow, some way, experience the unexplainable calm and the joy that God pours out, and may you swim in its depths—even in the darkest hours."

I've experienced those moments (sometimes seasons) of pain, in which I felt so empty and dark inside, I wondered if I would ever rejoice again. I've wept until I ached. And somehow, some way, in the midst of my grief, God revealed himself. A quiet, oh-so-subtle calm slowly moved over me. While the pain didn't disappear, the brutal edge of it lessened. God didn't "show up," as some would say, for he was there all along. He simply reminded me that I wasn't alone.

It seems that God has designed every

circumstance, every moment, as a reminder that we are not alone. When the sun rises each morning and the trees bear the beautiful, fresh, and stunning colors of spring, it's easy to remember and praise, along with the angels, "'Holy, holy, holy is the Lord of Heaven's Armies! The whole earth is filled with his glory!'" (Isaiah 6:3 NLT). But perhaps his glory is also to be found in the pain of death and loss and loneliness. Even in the darkest loneliness, he reminds us that although life continually changes, he doesn't. The earth and everything in it—including our private pain—is filled with his glory. He is the one—the only—constant. He is always there, never leaving us, never forgetting, never too busy, never sleeping. Never changing.

Maybe that's why life and the earth continually change—so we have a sharp contrast to the One who does not change (Malachi 3:6). And the One who does not change knows our names (John 10:3). He knows us intimately (Psalm 139:1–24). He loves us unabashedly and without end (1 John 3:1). He hears us (Psalm 55:17). He has compassion on us (Exodus 34:6) and comforts overwhelmingly. And nothing that happens in this life catches him off guard or by surprise (Ecclesiastes 7:14).

I visited my grandmother three weeks before she died. Until her final three-month stay in a nursing home, this eighty-nine-year-old woman—frail, fragile, widowed—lived alone in a big house in the country. She got out to attend church, check in with her doctor, and visit the beauty parlor. The rest of the time she lay on her couch and watched TV Land. Living two states away from her meant I couldn't visit as often as I'd liked. I worried that she spent so much time by herself—well, and with Ray Romano and Andy Griffith. I worried about her loneliness and wondered if she'd ever thought, *Time is passing. My husband is gone. And things will never be what they were.* I wondered if a sadness passed over her, missing life as it used to be. And I realized sharply again that God was with her during her marriage, and God was with her in her widowhood. Her circumstances changed, but he didn't. And that, too, is filled with his glory.

So that morning I sealed the envelope and mailed the sympathy card to my friend. I wiped my eyes of the tears over her loss, and over all our losses. I sighed and smiled a little, knowing that God was watching, in the room with me. He was in the room with my friend when she opened the card. He was in the room with my grandmother while she lay on her couch and sipped her iced tea, and then when she was moved to a nursing home. He was with her when she died. And he will be in the room with me when I am again overwhelmed by loss. And all those moments too will be filled with his glory: the glory of the unchanging Creator, Comforter, Almighty God, and Friend—who will never leave us alone.

With that knowledge I can then do as Paul encourages us: "Rejoice in the Lord always. I will say it again: Rejoice! . . . . The Lord is near" (Philippians 4:4–5 NIV).

How do we find happiness and rejoice when we struggle and suffer? When life will never be the same? When our dreams are gone? When the void threatens to overtake us?

And I know the answer.

The Lord is near.

He is near to the brokenhearted and "saves those who are crushed in spirit" (Psalm 34:18 NIV). We can rejoice because "the Lord is near."

Sara Hagerty expresses it this way:

For those of us with those dark places, who just can't muster up a thankfulness over the death of our father or the loss of a child or another birthday when we go to bed alone or the fact that we can't cover the mortgage. Again. Maybe we aren't meant to drum it up.

Maybe [God is] inviting us to crawl out of our conventional approach to him and ask to see his face. Maybe it's time for an emotional integrity before God we haven't yet allowed ourselves to have by quickly sweeping up the mess.

The nexus of our desire to be thankful and our inability to get there doesn't mean something is wrong with us, but instead it is our invitation. Maybe this is a chance to be vulnerably fascinated by God into thankfulness, even if our circumstances don't change.[7]

We don't need to chase after happiness when life is good. It's in these dark moments that we need joy to chase after us and embrace us with a fierceness. That's the invitation: to let go and ask God to meet us in our pain. To remind us that he is there, mourning with us.

And that is enough.

EMBRACING THE HAPPY LIFE:

- ❀ Are there hurts in your life that need healing? In your relationships?

- ❀ When was the last time you had a good cry? What was it about? How did you feel afterward?

- ❀ What loss have you struggled over? In what ways has it affected you?

- ❀ Have you ever thought about the healing power of music? In what ways do you think singing would help bring you a sense of peace?

WHAT THE BIBLE HAS TO SAY:

"Those who go out weeping, carrying seed to sow, will return with songs of joy" (Psalm 126:6 NIV).

WHAT'S IN IT FOR ME?

- ❀ Try singing. It doesn't have to be an upbeat, rah-rah song. Let it flow from your heart and offer it to God.

- ❀ Do a search through the Bible on how many people cry (from Esther to Jeremiah—the weeping prophet—to Peter). Give yourself permission to cry when you need to.

- ❀ This week, find a quiet place and talk to God aloud about your sorrow. Tell him about your hurts, your anger, your fears. Be honest with God—and with yourself.

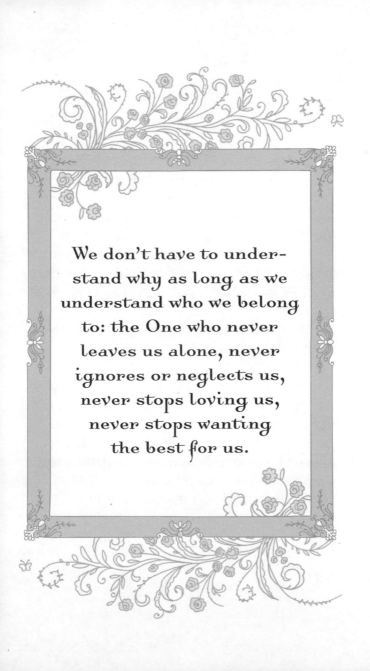

We don't have to under-
stand why as long as we
understand who we belong
to: the One who never
leaves us alone, never
ignores or neglects us,
never stops loving us,
never stops wanting
the best for us.

NOTES: CHAPTER 9

[1] From an account by Mary Livermore, a Boston schoolteacher in Virginia before the Civil War. http://www.christianity.com/church/church-history/timeline/1601-1700/slave-songs-transcend-sorrow-11630165.html.

[2] Karolyn Smardz Frost, *I've Got a Home in Glory Land: A Lost Tale of the Underground Railroad* (Macmillan, 2008), Google books, 102. https://books.google.com/books.

[3] As a side note, I think one of the coolest, most awe-inspiring sights is to see a man cry (not like mama's boy baby crying, but sincere crying).

[4] Barbara Westberg, "The Power of Tears," More to Life Bible Study Series.

[5] Ibid.

[6] Ibid.

[7] Sara Hagerty, "Waiting on Thankfulness: How God Works in Us during Times When We Can't Muster Gratitude," Her.meneutics, *Christianity Today*, November 25, 2014, http://www.christianitytoday.com/women/2014/november/waiting-on-thankfulness.html.

Chapter 10

TRYING ON THE SHOES MADE FOR YOU

*There are different kinds of gifts,
but the same Spirit distributes them.*

1 CORINTHIANS 12:4 NIV

Our sweet Cinderella has gone into hiding. She obediently left the ball as the clock struck midnight and as the spell wore off. But in her hasty exit, one of her glass slippers fell off. She was in such a rush that she was unable to retrieve it, leaving it on the staircase and limping ungracefully all the way back to her pumpkin coach.

But never fear, the prince grabbed it. Determined to make this mystery woman his bride, he made it his mission to find the shoe's owner ASAP. He sent his servants throughout the town and countryside, claiming, "If the shoe fits, he will commit."

Swooning girls everywhere held out a foot, ready to lay claim to the prince, his wealth, his kingdom, and his name. But no foot fit the slipper. In fact, in the Brothers Grimm version of the tale, just before the prince himself arrived at Cinderella's house, the stepmother advised her elder daughter to take whatever measure she could to ensure her foot was a slipper match. The best way to do that, *of course*, would be for the girl to cut off her toes.

The elder daughter, with no toes, placed her foot right into the shoe. Joy, oh joy! It fit. So away went the daughter with her low-IQed and observation-impaired prince. Clearly her continual wincing must have been from her excitement over her upcoming nuptials.

Since the prince failed to recognize what the stepsister had done, two doves had to fly down from heaven and alert the prince that blood dripped from his companion's foot. Horrified that he'd been the victim of such treachery—not to mention stupidity—he turned the carriage around, unceremoniously dumped sister #1, and turned his attention to sister #2. Not to be fooled again, he lifted her foot and checked this young woman's toes. Yep, all five there. Good sign.

He pulled out the glass slipper and—joy, oh joy!—it fit. Heaven be praised. He had found his beloved.

Unfortunately, as soon as sister #1 returned unmarried, Mama had quickly encouraged her other daughter to slice off part of her heel.

The doves again had to tweet the news:

> BLOOD ON THIS GIRL'S FOOT, TOO.
> CHECK WHERE HER HEEL USED TO BE.

Man, what is *it with these masochistic women?* the prince thought. *Well, third time's the charm, they say. Let's see if this household has any more eligible women.*

Seriously, at this point, I'm not sure I would have wanted to try another gal from that particular household, but the prince must have been an optimist, because once again, he showed up at Cinderella's house. Lo and behold, there was another girl—but she was a kitchen maid, a *cinder* girl. Surely the prince didn't want to waste his time trying to fit a shoe on the filthy, no-good servant.

"Well, I'm already here, so I might as well give it a try."

While the prince awaited her appearance, Cinderella quickly cleaned herself up and grabbed her other slipper as proof. She entered the room, gave a slight bow, and sat on the edge of her chair. The prince gave her foot a quick once-over—no blood, nothing missing. So he lifted her foot and smoothly eased it right into the shoe. Her foot nestled in perfectly.

She showed him the other shoe, to the horror and gasps of her step-relations, who bellowed their anger and frustration: "You mean I sliced up my foot for *nothing*?!"

Immediately, the prince recognized Cinderella as the beautiful stranger from the ball. He proposed. They married. . .and lived happily—and fully limbed—ever after.

The Great Happiness Stealers

Cinderella put her best foot forward to slide on the glass slipper that rightfully belonged to her. Likewise, God offers us wonderful, custom-made shoes that are created just for us. We have only to say yes. A big holdback, though? Too often we want so much to be Cinderella, but we become the ugly, bloodied-feet stepsisters. Jealousy and comparisons do a lot to steal our happiness.

We allow our happily ever afters to get crushed because we spend so much time looking at other people's happily ever afters, then we complain that ours aren't as good. The grass is greener and all that.

No wonder we struggle with happiness. How can we be truly happy when we don't have or can't get what others have?

I know the ultimate "Keep up with the Joneses" couple. They have the biggest, the best, the newest, the most recent toys. It doesn't matter what it is, they get it. One day while visiting me, the missus noticed that I had purchased a new computer.

"Wow, that's really nice!"

"Yeah, well, I had to get it. My other one died."

"Is it top of the line?" she asked.

"No, there's another level, but this is good enough for what I need."

Two weeks later when I visited her, there on her kitchen table sat her new computer—the top-of-the-line one.

"Here, let me show you how it works!" She

turned it on and gave me a tutorial on how much better it was than what I'd gotten. "I really didn't need a new computer, but this one is *so nice*."

The obvious here is that my friend sees what other people have and covets it—and then goes after it. She isn't happy unless she has what others have—or want. But as soon as she gets it, she's happy only briefly before she sees something else to covet.

The less obvious, though, is that I struggle with it, too.

All day long, my head can tell me that I don't need what she has, that I can't afford what she has, but I can still so easily become tempted to think, *Why* can't *I have those things? Why can't I have the nice house and the 2.5 kids, and the size 2 bod, and take the nice vacations? It isn't fair!*

And every time I get sucked into that kind of comparison thinking, my happiness turns sour and my perspective becomes minty green with envy.

What's worse, though, is that I can do the same comparison thinking in my professional life and with my relationships—and the worst of all, I can do it in my spiritual life!

I can compare my husband to someone else's: *My husband doesn't do that for me like her husband does.*

I can compare my parents to other parents: *My parents didn't go to all my band performances like her parents did.*

I can compare my job: *I've worked hard, why didn't I get that award?*

I can compare my coworkers: *I'm nice. Why don't my coworkers want to hang out with me like they do with her?*

It can sneak into every aspect of our lives. We compare our kids, our lifestyles, our cars, our hobbies. And where do we really get stuck in the comparison trap? Social media. Facebook and Pinterest are the scourge of the earth, in my humble opinion.

Our Digital Personas and the Lies We Believe

In the interest of full disclosure, I'm not a big fan of social media. Probably those previous two sentences gave that knowledge away. I have to do it for my work, but I tend to be more private, so I don't like to share a lot online. The truth is, though, that I can never think of anything worthwhile to share.

What if it isn't funny enough? Or profound enough? Or clever enough?

What if I don't look thin enough? Pretty enough?

Let's face it. How many posts or tweets have you read about some really stupid thing someone has done? Usually it's about what wonderful thing has happened. Or would you pray for this person who has some rare disease? It's either the really good stuff or the really bad stuff. Rarely is it the average stuff—the stuff that makes up 99.9 percent of our lives.

We edit our lives into a digital identity that we can control and that makes us appear to be better than we actually are. No negative traits there. No unflattering photos.

So the problem? That's what everybody else does, too. We are fooled into believing that everybody else's life is better than ours. We know that about social media, but we still believe the lie that the other people's social media persona is true.

"Social media puts an interesting lens on the creation of the self, and how this construction affects our mental well-being," writes Kelsey Sunstrum in "How Social Media Affects Our Self-Perception." She continues:

The ideal self is the self we aspire to be. My ideal self would be a 25-year-old successful freelance writer who lives in a perpetually clean house and who always takes the time to put on makeup before she leaves the house.

One's self-image is the person we actually are, based on the actions, behaviors, and habits currently possessed. My self-image would be of a 25-year-old freelance writer just starting her business in a house that's mostly clean most of the time and who forces herself not to wear pajamas everywhere.[1]

When we buy into the social media lies, it has a devastating effect on our happiness levels. And studies prove it.

For two weeks, researchers at the University of Michigan sent text messages to eighty-two Ann Arbor residents five times a day. They wanted to learn how people felt overall: how worried and lonely they were, how much they had used Facebook, and how often they'd interacted with others between each text message. They found that the more the subjects used Facebook in the time between the texts, the less happy they felt. Their analysis: Facebook makes people unhappy.[2]

Over and over studies have shown the same thing: the more we use social media, the more lonely, disconnected, and unhappy we feel. One study even concluded that Facebook could cause problems in relationships by increasing feelings of jealousy.[3] The more time people spend reading about other people's successes, the more envious they feel, causing social comparison. Since your friends on Facebook generally share similarities with you, learning about their achievements can be a harder hit. "We want to learn about other people and have others learn about us," says Maria Konnikova in her *New Yorker* article "How Facebook Makes Us Unhappy," "but through that very learning process we may start to resent both others' lives and the image of ourselves that we feel we need to continuously maintain."[4]

In a sense, we cut off our toes to fit into what we covet.

As we consume more of the lies, we can begin to process what we read and see with a negative bias, which then validates our faulty thinking. Consider this: the photos, the recipes, the posts, and the tweets—how many of them glamorize another person's life? So what happens? You see them, you process it through a faulty belief, and it leads you to minimize the positives in your own life. Even though you *know* that those things have been carefully crafted to present the person in a certain light.

"Often people who are depressed or

anxious set themselves up to feel worse by falling prey to their self-fulfilling prophecies that they're worthless or not liked," says Stephanie Mihalas, a psychologist and a clinical instructor in the department of psychiatry and biobehavioral sciences at the David Geffen School of Medicine at UCLA.[5]

It's time to stop slicing our own feet to fit into someone else's life shoes and nestle into the shoes meant for us.

So What Are Our Shoes?

Cinderella would never have gotten to her happily ever after had she not allowed the prince to place the shoe on her foot. But she said yes. Because she knew that shoe was hers. It was made for her. And by wearing that slipper, it opened the door for her to gain access to all the rights and privileges of becoming royalty.

We have shoes made for us. And when we say yes to wearing those shoes—our shoes—we also gain access to all the rights and privileges of royalty.

So what are our shoes?

- ❧ Understanding and embracing who we truly are in Christ—who he made us to be

- ❧ Discovering the gifts and skills that he has carefully crafted and given us and using them to honor God

- ❧ Living out our calling with joy—in the midst of pain and suffering. Holding on to Jesus—even when he feels absent or when we're not sure that he is working on our behalf

- ❧ Sharing what Jesus has done for us

It's time to put on your shoes, my friend. But to do that, you need to do a few things:

1. IT'S TIME TO GIVE UP THE LIE THAT SAYS "I'M NOT AS WORTHY OF GOD'S LOVE AS OTHER CHRISTIANS ARE."

There are moments when I think, *I'm a fake. I'm not pleasing God. At some point, someone's going to realize that. Then everybody will see that I'm not as good as everybody else.* Do you ever do that?

My friend Jane Struck admitted to believing this lie.

> *For many years I've struggled with the gut feeling that compared to everyone*

else, I'm negligible in God's eyes. Unfortunately, this belief pervaded my relationship with him and with others, as well as impugned my ability to plunge into whole-hearted service. So in an effort to compensate for my perceived inadequacies, I've tried to earn love by being "nice"—someone who's caring and kind and sweet, who tries not to rock the boat or upset anyone.

I cringe to think of the years I've allowed this faulty belief to influence me. The reality is, it. . .has no biblical basis on which to stand. I continually need to surrender this lie to the truth God loves me (John 3:16), rejoices over me (Zephaniah 3:17), died for me (Romans 5:8), and will never leave or forsake me (Romans 8:39). That means he loves me when I'm nice—and when I'm not. He loves me even when others don't.

I may never be a beautiful, popular, recognizable, and successful woman in this world, but worldly labels, accolades, recognition, and accomplishments hold no sway over God's irrational love for me. I've been beholden to the deception that others

are more special than I am for way too
long. I need to remember: we're all
equals at the cross.[6]

Because of what Christ did for us, we absolutely are worthy of God's love. And God heaps, smothers, overloads that love on us. Look at what the apostle John tells us:

See what great love the Father has
lavished on us, that we should be called
children of God! And that is what we are!
1 JOHN 3:1 NIV

Read that verse again and let it sink in. You are a child of the living God. He doesn't just love you, he *lavishes* his love on you. It's time to start living as though you truly believe that.

2. IT'S TIME FOR US TO WEAR THE SHOES THAT BELONG TO US—NOT TO SOMEBODY ELSE.

The stepsisters sure tried to cram their feet into Cinderella's shoes. Didn't fit. They forced their feet to create an unnatural fit. But sometimes we try to do that, don't we?

We look at what somebody else is doing with their life. We see the blessings other people have, and envy can begin to seep into our souls.

The sweet Liz Curtis Higgs, a *New York Times* bestselling author, world traveler, and renowned speaker, has struggled with professional jealousy. When she became a writer, she found herself attending conferences and mingling with other writers and wondering,

"How come she's moving along faster than I am, Lord? Why did they honor her instead of me?" I wasn't jealous, of course. Merely, uh. . .competitive.

The awful truth revealed itself one gray morning when I received an announcement from a colleague who'd been blessed with an opportunity I was convinced should have been mine. I tossed the letter across the room in an angry huff, whining, "It's not fair, Lord!"

He chose that moment to get my attention. "Was the cross of Calvary fair, Liz? Have I called you to succeed—or surrender?"

I was undone. Jealousy, envy, and strife were alive and well in my jade-green heart.[7]

I see this a lot when I attend conferences or get together with other people in my profession. And I've struggled with my share of the same competitive, green-eyed monster.

In some cases, it's good to compare because it helps us strive to be better. For instance, Paul tells us to follow his example as he follows Christ's (1 Corinthians 11:1).

It turns ugly, though, when we want to overtake that example. As Mark Twain says, "Comparison is the death of joy."

Happiness and comparisons rarely survive or thrive in the same breath.

I've heard people complain because they didn't get the same attention as some other worship singer got. That someone else's kids are smarter, cooler, funnier. That they're just a stay-at-home mom and this other person has an exciting job and gets to travel.

I've even heard people complain about their spiritual gifts! When I was editor of *Today's Christian Woman,* we ran a special section on spiritual gifts. I was stunned when I received e-mails from women who complained about the gifts they had: "I wish I had a cooler spiritual gift. Something like teaching. Instead my gift is administration. How lame is that?" *Forgive us, Lord, for thinking we know how to divvy up the gifts better than you do.*

Why do we compare and want somebody else's _____? We're not on their path. We have our own path to walk.

In John 21, we read a great passage about

how Jesus responds to comparisons.

After Jesus was resurrected, he appeared to the disciples by the Sea of Galilee. Jesus had just cooked them some freshly caught fish and they had eaten their fill. He turned his attention to Peter, who had earlier denied knowing him three times.

Jesus asked Peter three times, "Do you love me?"

Each time Peter told him, "Yes, Lord, you know that I love you."

And Jesus responded, "Feed my sheep." The third time, he added a prophecy about Peter:

> *"Very truly I tell you, when you were younger you dressed yourself and went where you wanted; but when you are old you will stretch out your hands, and someone else will dress you and lead you where you do not want to go." Jesus said this to indicate the kind of death by which Peter would glorify God. Then he said to him, "Follow me!"*
> JOHN 21:17–19 NIV

Jesus had just told Peter an important piece of prophecy. He gave him a clear and direct calling. And what did Peter do? He compared. He looked over at John, who was minding his own business, and said, "Lord, what about him? What is his life going to be?"

He wasn't really interested in John's life; he wanted to know how his life and death would measure up to John's. Would it be better? Worse? His prophesied death didn't sound too pleasant—and he wanted to make sure John's wouldn't be either.

I love Jesus' response here—because it's so convicting. It reminds me of my place in his kingdom.

> *Jesus answered, "If I want him to remain alive until I return, what is that to you? You must follow me."*
> JOHN 21:22 NIV

Peter had just received forgiveness and a calling. Jesus had just told him, "Hey, we're cool. Now let's get back on point. I want you to grow my people, strengthen them, take care of them. Oh, and by the way, that's going to lead you to a pretty difficult death. But through it all, I want you to follow me completely."

Wow, can you imagine getting that kind of message about what you're supposed to do with the rest of your life?

Peter was just given a huge gift. And he took it and threw it back in Christ's face. "But what about *him*?" (I imagine he said it kind of whiny.)

We do that. *I wish I had that spiritual gift. I wish I had a vocation, not just a job. My life is miserable; why isn't hers miserable, too?*

We each have different paths. Where God has called and placed me isn't where God has called and placed you. And vice versa.

The writer of Hebrews reminds us to run the race that God has set out for each of us. If we want to compare, he continues, we should fix our eyes on Jesus, who is the author of our life story, of our faith. When we do that, it's much easier for us to be content with who we are and where we are and to rejoice when others succeed. Because they're doing what God called them to do.

We're positioned right where God has us for this place and time and purpose. You can do something that I never can. God meant for it to be that way.

3. IT'S TIME FOR US TO EMBRACE OUR GIFTS AND EMBRACE WHO GOD MADE US TO BE.

Christians have the corner on cheesy statements. So what kind of Christian book can I write if I don't include one? There's a saying that was popular a few decades ago that went like this: "You are created in the image of God, and God doesn't make junk!"

Totally cheesy. But it's true.

God formed you. He gave you a personality and sense of humor (or lack of one). He gave you something that nobody else has. He assigned it to you. And only you.

There's a great Christmas song that says, "Why me, I'm just a simple man of trade? . . . Why her, she's just an ordinary girl? . . . This is such a strange way to save the world."[8] Of all the people God could have chosen to be parents for his Son, he chose a carpenter and a teenage girl.

That's overwhelming to me! And when I think about the skills and gifts God has put within me to use for him, I think, *Why me? You chose to give me these blessings. You trust me with them. What a strange way to build your kingdom.* It's sobering and amazing and thrilling!

That means we don't have to compare. We may not be the best at something, but it doesn't matter! Because "if the willingness is there, the gift is acceptable according to what one has, not according to what one does not have" (2 Corinthians 8:12 NIV). And that gift fits perfectly with how God has gifted other people. Paul tells us that "there are different kinds of gifts, but the same Spirit distributes them" (1 Corinthians 12:4 NIV).

Several years ago, I met an interior decorator who told me she really struggled with the idea of vocation, because she didn't feel as if she was really doing anything for God by decorating rich people's houses. I started to ask her about her clients, and she told me about one whom she'd started to talk with. She got to know her client and told her about church and the Bible.

"That's your gift!" I told her. "You're reaching and influencing someone whom a pastor can't reach. Do you think maybe God gave you a designer's eye so that you can connect and relate with people outside the church?"

Her mouth dropped and then her face lit up. "I've never thought about it that way!"

Embrace the gifts God has given you. They are special. And he has planned special ways for you to use them.

4. IT'S TIME FOR US TO SAY NO TO SOME THINGS.

I've discovered in my own life that one of the best tools of the enemy is to keep us busy. And distracted. Even in the midst of doing God's work. But sometimes God doesn't want us to *do*. He wants us to *be*. We discussed this in a previous chapter, but I think it's important enough to revisit here.

We give to our children, our spouses, our friends, our jobs, our churches. We don't have anything left! Practice saying no—for every no you say, you say yes to something else. Make that yes to God. And he will fill you.

Just sit and wait on God. Listen. Enjoy who he is. Just *be* and relish the love that he lavishes on you. James tells us to "draw near to God, and he will draw near to you" (James 4:8 ESV). In *The Message*, he says, "Say a quiet *yes* to God and he'll be there in no time." But you can only do that by saying no, by setting your priorities. By asking God to show you what needs to stay and what needs to go.

The more clear we become on what gets a no and what gets a yes, the happier and more confident we will find ourselves.

5. IT'S TIME TO STOP WORRYING ABOUT WHAT YOU CAN'T CONTROL AND FOCUS ON LIVING IN THE MOMENT.

I know crazy people who do this insane thing called running a marathon. I don't understand the allure to putting your body through that kind of torture. But for whatever reason, they insist on doing it. One woman I know has run the Chicago marathon every year for the past ten years.

She will tell you, as crazy as she is, that people who run a marathon don't start training by going out and running 26.2 miles the first time out. They spend months training and building up to it. Every week it's a little bit longer, until by the end of the training, they're finally running the full amount.

A novelist doesn't sit down and, in one sitting, write an entire book. It's a chapter or a set amount of words at a time. If she tried to write a novel at one time, she'd probably pass out from the thought of it. It's too big of a project. And she'd quit not too far into it.

The old saying goes, "How do you eat an elephant? One bite at a time." (I think it's kind of a stupid saying, since who would eat an elephant?) But the point is, we need to take one bite, one step, one moment at a time.

I can't control my future, and if I spend all my time worrying over that, then I lose my happiness. What can I control? That's simple: I can control how I choose to respond and live in the moment right here and now. I can no longer control the past—it's gone. I don't need to control the future—it isn't here yet. But *this* moment? I can choose to accept it, to lean into it, to appreciate it for what it is and what it can teach me, to enjoy it.

What makes us be able to live in the moment? Two verses come to mind:

❧ "We are more than conquerors [or overcomers]" (Romans 8:37 NIV). Another translation says that "overwhelming victory is ours through Christ, who loved us" (NLT).

❧ "For God has not given us a spirit of fear and timidity, but of power, love, and self-discipline" (2 Timothy 1:7 NLT).

We waste so much time and energy trying to figure out so many things that we don't know. We don't know the mind of God—we take one page of our story at a time by faith. We trust that Jesus, who is the author of our faith, is a really good writer. And he knows the ending.

The shoes sit there, waiting for you. Don't cut off your toes and slice your heel to try to squeeze into someone else's shoes. Yours are tailor made. And they're pretty doggone cool. So put them on. Your happiness—your life—depends on it.

EMBRACING THE HAPPY LIFE:

❀ What beliefs about yourself do you need to surrender to Christ? What beliefs about God do you need to surrender to Christ? What beliefs about others do you need to surrender to Christ?

❀ Think about how much you use social media. What do you get out of it? How do you feel when you use it? Is there a way to use those sites in a more productive way?

❀ Is there someone to whom you compare yourself often? Why? In what aspects can you let the comparisons go and embrace your own unique and treasured identity?

❀ What holds you back from seeing the beauty and value in your own life? Do you ever assume it's inferior to your idealized version of someone else's life? If so, why?

WHAT'S IN IT FOR ME?

- Put some boundaries in place for when and how you'll use social media.

- When you do use social media, if you find that you start to feel envious or compare your life with someone else's, confront those attitudes and thoughts and question their validity.

- Confess and pray. First, admit that jealousy is a sin: "If you harbor bitter envy and selfish ambition in your hearts, do not boast about it or deny the truth" (James 3:14 NIV). Then ask for forgiveness and healing. Pray for a clean heart.

- Celebrate other people's successes. Remembering that each of us has our own unique path helps me genuinely celebrate other people's successes. It's not as if the success pool is limited. When one person succeeds, God doesn't provide less to go around. There's room enough for everyone to succeed—in the way God has designed.

- When you hear about something good happening to another person, shoot them an e-mail or call them or send them an actual piece of mail to say, "Way to go!"

✿ Keep focused. When you compare yourself to another person, you aren't spending the time where it could be better spent: on your own calling. I love what one woman said: "What others do is God's business, not mine." Amen, sista.

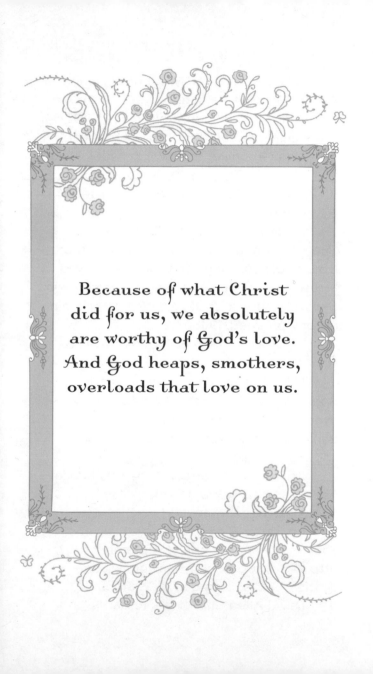

Because of what Christ did for us, we absolutely are worthy of God's love. And God heaps, smothers, overloads that love on us.

[1] Kelsey Sunstrum, "How Social Media Affects Our Self-Perception," 2014, http://psychcentral.com/blog/archives/2014/03/14/how-social-media-affects-our-self-perception/.

[2] Maria Konnikova, "How Facebook Makes Us Unhappy," *The New Yorker*, September 10, 2013, http://www.newyorker.com/tech/elements/how-facebook-makes-us-unhappy.

[3] Muise A, Christofides E, Desmarais S. "More Information Than You Ever Wanted: Does Facebook Bring Out the Green-Eyed Monster of Jealousy?" *Cyberpsychology and Behavior,* August 2009, http://www.ncbi.nlm.nih.gov/pubmed/19366318.

[4] Konnikova, "How Facebook Makes Us Unhappy."

[5] Mikel Theobald, "Depression and Social Media," May 29, 2014, http://www.everydayhealth.com/health-report/major-depression-resource-center/depression-social-media.aspx.

[6] Jane Johnson Struck, "The Lies I Believe," *Today's Christian Woman* blog, March 3, 2009. [Has since been removed.]

[7] Liz Curtis Higgs, "Who, Me? Jealous?" *Today's Christian Woman*, September 1997, http://www.todayschristianwoman.com/articles/1997/september/7w5060.html.

[8] David Allen Clark, Mark R. Harris, and

Donald A. Koch. "A Strange Way to Save the World," New Spring Publishing Inc., http://www.azlyrics.com/lyrics/fredhammond/astrangewaytosavetheworld.html.

Chapter 11

OUR HAPPILY EVER AFTER

*The steadfast love of the L*ORD *never ceases, his mercies never come to an end; they are new every morning.*

LAMENTATIONS 3:22-23 NRSV

Once upon a time. . .

In a kingdom, not unlike your own neighborhood, lived a lovely woman who had a heart of compassion and kindness. She tried to live a good and healthy life. She treated others as she desired to be treated. She kept a moderately clean house, paid her bills on time, and didn't kick cats, dogs, birds, or small children. She sang while filling her dishwasher and hummed a sweet little tune while folding clothes and brushing her teeth.

And when her family didn't appreciate her or her neighbors irritated, frustrated, and generally annoyed her, she held her tongue and chose to love them anyway (although she did have moments when she gave in to the passing rant).

She may never have won a beauty contest, *American Idol*, or Publisher's Clearinghouse, but that was okay by her. She knew who she was: a princess whose Father lavished love and mercy on her. And she lived confidently within that understanding.

Every morning she arose from her slumber, ready to greet the day and all that was in it. She asked her Father to bless her that day with enough strength to face any obstacles, challenges, or adversaries. And she chose to walk into that day's adventure with a fierce commitment to see her Father's work and fingerprints all over everything and then to hug the happiness and gratitude in every moment presented to her.

Her life was not perfect. At times she struggled to hold her head up when the day— sometimes the season—offered intense sorrow and imperfections. But she remained true to her calling: to live the life that her Father planned for her—using her unique skills and personality—and to share her happiness and thanksgiving with others around her, rejoicing or weeping with them.

With each day that passed, she matured and recognized more easily the moments of joy that presented themselves. She remained faithful to her Father. And he continued to overwhelm her with the best treasures from his kingdom.

And she lived happily ever after every day.

We Have a Choice

That really does sound like a fairy tale, doesn't it? But it can be your fairy tale—it can be your reality. God has a beautiful story for you. It's a love story that has his fingerprints all over every single page.

Too often we try to make our lives so complicated—and they truly don't have to be. We have everything we need to live a successful, happy life. Paul reminds us that "in everything we have won more than a victory because of Christ who loves us" (Romans 8:37 CEV). But it's up to us. How will we choose to write our life story?

Will we choose to make it one of joy—even in the midst of sorrow? Will we make sure that the Father plays a leading role? Or will we allow the evil witch to tempt us with the poisoned apple, and fall into a deep sleep?

Will we allow ourselves to grasp and believe that God is madly in love with us and will pursue us without abandon? That even when we make mistakes, we will continue to run to him, because we know that his love is steadfast and never ceases, and his "mercies never come to an end; they are new every morning" (Lamentations 3:22–23 NRSV)?

We are not a mistake. We are a precious treasure. And we have the choice: we can believe our *true* worth and fill our minds with God's Word and live out the story he has written for us, or we can choose to live the story that the enemy of our souls wants to write for us—the one that will fill our minds with lies.

We get to decide.

Fortunately, we don't have to make that choice alone. God promises to help us.

When God appeared to Moses in a burning bush and gave him the 411 on his plan to free his people from slavery, Moses gave every excuse he could.

"I can't do that for you, Lord. Sorry, I'd love to help you out, but, you know, I don't think so well on my feet and I'm a terrible public speaker. I stutter and say stupid things. Really, I'm not your go-to guy."

And God replied to Moses with a message that applies to us as well:

> *"Who makes a person's mouth? Who decides whether people speak or do not speak, hear or do not hear, see or do not see? Is it not I, the Lord? Now go! I will be with you as you speak, and I will instruct you in what to say."*
> Exodus 4:11–12 NLT

"I will be with you. . .I will instruct you. . . ."

We are not alone in this journey. God will help us and he will provide everything we need to write a bestselling life story.

What to Keep in Mind

As we write our life stories to be filled with happily ever afters, we need to keep a few things in mind. These will help us to maintain a clear perspective.

1. CHALLENGES ARE PART OF LIFE.

Struggles are natural to this life. You won't be exempt. So it's okay to understand that your life is not going to be without pitfalls and hurdles.

We do a grave disservice to ourselves and to others when we suggest that the Christian life should be without troubles.

Just last night I was at a gathering for twentysomethings in which we were discussing the movie *Old Fashioned*, my companion book *The Old Fashioned Way*, and *Fifty Shades of Grey*. We essentially were looking at two very different options for how to handle and navigate relationships.

After a bit of toying with going deeper, one brave young woman finally said what everyone had been thinking (I know this because they all nodded and uttered their agreement).

"I've messed up a lot in my relationships, and I don't feel as if anybody has given me permission to really struggle or to share what I'm struggling with. I feel as if I'm being judged if I'm not perfect."

That sets us all up for a heaping pile of failure and a constant barrage of "Why me?" questions.

Trouble *will* come to us. We must plan on it. Prepare for it. Be on the lookout for it. As we progress through life, we will learn quickly that the way the story begins—what we think will or should happen—is rarely how the story will actually play out.

Sometimes the trouble comes because we bring it on ourselves. Mostly it comes because we live in a fallen world with a bunch of broken people. We need not be surprised when trouble comes; we can acknowledge it, ask God to help us through it; and grow more mature because of it. Then when the next problem comes along, we'll be a little wiser and even more prepared to face it. That's what becoming Christlike is all about.

Don't take it personally; it's the nature of our fallen world. But if we stay focused on God's story for us rather than on the trouble or challenge, we will experience happily ever after.

2: PEOPLE NEED TO READ YOUR STORY.

Too often we keep our life stories close to our vest. We get vulnerable in our friendships and other relationships—but only to a point. We talk about being authentic and genuine—but that really applies more for the other person. We'll only be as authentic and genuine as we feel comfortable being.

Last night after the first twentysomething spoke up, another woman became vulnerable and admitted, "I don't even completely share what I'm going through with my friends because I think they'll judge me."

"What if sharing our messiness is the path to growth and strength and happiness?" I asked. "It's scary! But what if part of God's plan for us is to share the messiness and the discomfort in that because someone else needs to know the reality of struggles, that they aren't alone, and that there's hope?"

The truth is that God works through our messiness—not only for our sakes but to help and encourage others as well. I'll be the first to admit that I've messed up more times than "Let It Go" has played on every young girl's iPod. But I've also experienced forgiveness and hope for a brighter future—and that makes me want to share with others that they have that same freedom available to them.

We need to share our life story—but that means we have to be honest about our own pain.

I have a friend who had a terribly abusive

first marriage. She's happily remarried now but refuses to talk about it. She has a national platform. What a waste of an opportunity. She could encourage and strengthen so many women, but she won't go there.

I understand it's painful. And I'm not suggesting she get on Twitter and Facebook and *The View* and share all the gory details, but she can be a beacon of hope and help to others just by being honest. But there's something else to sharing our story: it provides us healing as well.

Many years ago, I met a woman who wanted to write an article about how you could use the principles of dog training to "train" your husband. (No comment on that one.) It was technically well written but kind of bland. What grabbed my attention in the article was that she mentioned being adopted as an older child. Since that's so unusual, I asked her about it and discovered that she and her mother and siblings fled from Germany to the United States during World War II. Her mother was unable to care for the kids, so this woman had been adopted.

"What happened to your father?"

She shook her head. "I haven't seen or spoken to him since I left Germany."

"Really?" I waited for her to continue. Finally, when I realized she wasn't going to, I persisted—because I'm really nosy and sensed that she had a fascinating story. "Why haven't you reconnected with him?"

She admitted that she hadn't because he was an SS officer with the Nazis and she'd found out that he committed atrocities. "I had no desire once I learned who he really was."

I sat back amazed. She had this unbelievable life story—and she wanted to write about dog training principles? Don't get me wrong, I'm a huge animal lover, but I can read a dog/husband training article anytime. What I can't get is a story about a woman who struggled with having a father who was an SS soldier in World War II and trying to come to grips with having a parent who hurt others.

She had a story no one else could tell. I sensed that even in her senior years, she'd been unable to really come to terms with it. But what if she'd decided to take a risk and tell other people? What might have happened? Perhaps the ability to forgive? To move on? And then to help others who struggle?

When we keep safe and don't allow other people to read the difficult chapters of our lives—even when they make us feel uncomfortable—then we miss God-given opportunities, but also, we miss the healing that Jesus can bring to our stories. We miss the joy that comes when we refuse to allow our pain and our failures to hold us hostage.

Remember that everyone has struggles. So when you allow others to see the painful parts of you, God can open doors to your healing and then comfort and encourage those other folks. You can become a vehicle for their healing.

Share your story. You don't have to give every detail. But take the risk and be vulnerable.

3. JOY IS FOUND IN THE JOURNEY, BUT WE HAVE TO GRASP ON TO IT.

Too often we confuse joy with happiness. Happiness is wonderful. God purposefully gave us that emotion—and I happen to really like it. And I find I am generally a happy person. But happiness—as does every emotion—comes and goes. If I find a dress that's on super sale and looks great on me, I'm happy. If the mirrors in the dressing room make me feel as if I'm in the house of horrors, I'm not so happy.

While happiness is great, I'm much more interested in joy. Joy sticks around when happiness takes a vacation. Why? Because joy is a byproduct of allowing the Holy Spirit to control our lives—it is what the apostle Paul calls a fruit of the Spirit (Galatians 5:22–23). Joy is not dependent upon our circumstances.

Several years ago, I spoke with speaker and

author Thelma Wells on the idea of joy. I asked her why some Christians don't seem to have joy.

"Can you lose it?"

No, she assured me. "But it sure can go underground."

A lot of Christians are walking around with their joy buried.

During that period of my life in which I was dealing with difficult issues with work and in my personal life, I grew angry at God. I felt as though he was withholding from me. And one evening I found myself, in the midst of pouring out my anger, feeling a sense of joy. Not happiness. Joy. In my anger I began to say aloud, "But you are a good God. You are a good God. And I love you."

I began to think of David writing his psalms. He would pour out his anguish to God—honestly, vulnerably—and only when he'd spent himself would he begin to say, "But where can I go from you? You are my life. I will yet praise you."

Happiness is like the fireworks during the Fourth of July. Big and wonderful and exciting and showy. Joy is the quiet calm of being at peace in the midst of every situation—knowing that God has it under control, that he has a plan for us, and it involves goodness and not disaster, and a hope-filled future (Jeremiah 29:11). That is the promise of happily ever after.

Are You Ready?

You want to live happily ever after right now? You can.

Your life matters. You have potential. God wants to use your life, your pain, your messed-up moments, your regrets, your shame, your celebration, your heartache. Right now. Not later, not after you've tried to figure everything out on your own. Right. Now. Because that's what makes the happily ever after so sweet.

If Cinderella's story went like this—"Once upon a time, Cinderella and her father had a great relationship and her stepmother was a bastion of love and affection, and one day Cinderella met the prince and they lived happily ever after. The end."—she never would have grown, she never would have been able to appreciate the rescue from her life of drudgery.

God wants to use our life story. He wants to bring us both happiness and holiness. They are both connected.

If you really think about it, your life isn't just a story. God wants it to be a page-turner. Every day, you can ask God, *What are you going to bring into my life today, God, that will make me a stronger person? A better Christian? Someone who's closer to you? Someone who can help others?*

Believe me, that's a prayer God will answer. He presents those adventures to you every single day.

Have you forgotten about the joy that God has designed as part of your journey?

Are you allowing the challenges that are part of life to make you lose your focus on the ending?

Are you allowing yourself to get swallowed up in the pain instead of using it, refocusing it into what can ultimately become a positive outcome? Both for you and for others?

Have you allowed opportunities of ministry to go by because of fear of being vulnerable?

God has a beautiful story for you. As you say yes—to the dress, to the dwarfs, to the journey—I hope you'll discover new things about yourself that will leave you breathless, wondrously in awe, and overwhelmed with an inexplicable peace, insight, and wisdom. There's no time like the present to get started. You don't have to wait for your "real" life to begin; it's begun, baby!

Happily ever after is not a fairy tale; it is a choice. I believe you'll choose wisely and live in the light of Christ's love, healing, and restoration. So that every day you'll awaken, ready to meet the adventure of the day, and know that you and God are living happily ever after right now.

The
End.

YOUR HAPPILY-EVER-AFTER RULES RECAP

- ✿ It is possible to be happy and holy. Just make sure you strike a healthy balance.

- ✿ Beware of poisoned apples. They will distract you and keep you from your pursuit of happiness.

- ✿ Pick the right people to surround yourself with. Your team needs to be trustworthy and honest with you. They need to hold you accountable. If they aren't, get different teammates.

- ✿ Faith and resilience take work—but are worth the pursuit. Whenever you make a mistake, get back in the race and focus on your future success.

- ✿ Seize the day! Take a chance and risk rather than play it safe. No princess ever got ahead by sitting back and waiting for happiness to show up.

- ✿ Look beyond the outward appearance and first impressions. Give people the benefit of the doubt and second shots. You may acquire some great relationships when you give people opportunities to show you their beautiful traits.

- ❀ You are a beautiful swan. Embrace your God-given, God-loved identity and start living like one.

- ❀ You've been invited into a regular Sabbath rest. Take it.

- ❀ Don't allow the past to keep you from living fully in the present. The past is just that: the past. Do not let it hold you hostage and keep you from being all God wants you to be.

- ❀ You were created for a special purpose. God has great plans specific to the way he created you. So stop checking out what other people are doing and comparing your life to theirs. There's plenty of room for everyone to live successfully and happily.

- ❀ Happily ever after is a choice, not a fairy tale. Decide today to choose happiness— but even more so, to pursue joy.

Acknowledgments

everal years ago, the **Florida Women of the Church of God** invited me to speak at their annual retreat. The topic: Happily Ever After. The scripture passages: Hebrews. I scratched my head in wonder, trying to determine how in the world to connect Disney princesses with the graduate-level scriptures that make up the book of Hebrews.

One woman told me, "Do you have a book on this stuff? You really should." I smiled and mentally tucked it away and went back to my job and all the other tremendously important issues of life. And then one day her words came back to me when I began to notice more and more women struggling to gain a modicum of happiness—me being one of them. *Maybe I should write all this down,* I thought.

And so I owe these Florida CHOG women a huge debt of gratitude. In particular **Lois Linamen,** who has the patience of a saint— especially when she kept contacting me and I was way too slow to respond. **Angie Rigdon,** whom I rudely lost contact with but whom I enjoyed tremendously. And to one of the conferees who sent me a lovely handmade item and whom I neglected to send a thank-you to. Thank you. I smile whenever I think of you. And I think of you all often.

I also owe a big thank-you to **Annie Tipton,** my delightful and wonderful editor (who also knows the best kind of iced tea drink concoctions around). You caught the vision of this book from the start and we've had fun shaping it. And to **Shalyn Sattler**, **Brigitta Nortker**, and the rest of the Barbour team, thank you, thank you for your amazing work. You make me look *so good*!

Thank you to **Mary Keeley.** I'm grateful not only that you're my literary agent, but also that I can call you friend.

I could never write a book that has Disney and princesses in it without at least somewhere acknowledging my dear friend and uber Disney fan, **Dawn Zemke.** Dawn, I'm ready for another whirlwind trip through the Magic Kingdom—this time I'll try to be healthy for it.

Drew Dyck. Thank you for finding the Martin Luther cartoon caption for me. Per our conversation and my promise: I hereby dedicate this paragraph to you. I also fought long and hard to get your face on the book's cover, but those publishing house editors can beat me at arm wrestling every time.

Scott, Mom, Dad, and Ruby. I couldn't love you more—unless you stopped asking what's for dinner, when are you coming over, and would you take me outside to potty (respectively speaking).

My real Prince Charming. I'm so grateful you fitted my foot with the glass slipper, gave me true love's kiss, and defeated the evil one. I do not deserve such joy, my Savior, but am so deeply awed that you continue to pursue me, shaping me into your likeness until the day when I see you as you are, and I will be completely like you: perfect. But I promise not to brag about that.

About the Author

Ginger Kolbaba is an accomplished, award-winning author, editor, and speaker. She has written or contributed to more than twenty books, including the Gold Medallion–nominated *Refined by Fire* (which also received a starred review in *Publishers' Weekly*), the Golden Scroll–nominated *Until We All Come Home*, and her novel series Secrets from Lulu's Café. She is a contributing writer for *Thriving Family* magazine and has been a columnist for *Let's Worship*. She has published more than 400 magazine and online articles.

Ginger's heart is with women of all ages. Her greatest fun is when she can help them mature in their faith. In the publishing industry for almost two decades (she started very young), Ginger has been able to accomplish that in a number of different ways. She is the former editor of *Today's Christian Woman* magazine, *Marriage Partnership* magazine, and the founding editor of Kyria.com, all award-winning resources of Christianity Today. She has spoken at national and international conferences, guest lectured at college campuses, and has appeared on national media outlets such as CNN Headline News (Nancy Grace), Court TV, Moody Midday Connection, and Family Life radio. She's been quoted in national news outlets such as *Newsweek* and *Chicago Sun-Times*.

Ginger graduated summa cum laude with a BA in pre-law/American Studies and a double minor in theatre arts and Bible. After graduation she worked as a professional actress/singer (and in three shows in which she tap danced). Now a full-time writer, speaker, and editor, she still occasionally dons her tap shoes and shuffles over her hardwood floors. . .much to the dismay of her husband and dog.

Visit her at www.gingerkolbaba.com